COVID-19 AND THE FINANCE SECTOR IN ASIA AND THE PACIFIC

GUIDANCE NOTE

DECEMBER 2021

ASIAN DEVELOPMENT BANK

ADB

© 2021 Asian Development Bank
6 ADB Avenue, Mandaluyong City, 1550 Metro Manila, Philippines
Tel +63 2 8632 4444; Fax +63 2 8636 2444
www.adb.org

Some rights reserved. Published in 2021.

ISBN 978-92-9269-322-0 (print); 978-92-9269-323-7 (electronic); 978-92-9269-324-4 (ebook)
Publication Stock No. TIM210532-2
DOI: http://dx.doi.org/10.22617/TIM210532-2

Notes:
In this publication, "$" refers to the United States dollar, "AMD" refers to dram, "B" refers to baht, "CNY" refers to yuan, "D" refers to dong, "GEL" refers to lari, "HK$" referts to Hong Kong dollar, "₹" refers to Indian rupee, "₱" refers to peso, "RM" refers to ringgit, "Rp" refers to rupiah, "S$" refers to Singapore dollar, "SLRe" refers to Sri Lanka rupee, "T" refers to tenge, "Tk" refers to taka, and "W" refers to won.
ADB recognizes "China" as the People's Republic of China; "Hong Kong" as Hong Kong, China; "Korea" as the Republic of Korea; "Siam" as Thailand; and "Vietnam" as Viet Nam.

On the cover: (1) Hafiz Mohsin is recharging his Zu card himself from recharging machine on BRT station. ADB supported for safe, modern urban transport services where people travel easily in Peshawar, Pakistan (photo by Rahim Mirza/ADB). (2) People doing bank transactions during the COVID-19 pandemic in Cambodia (photo by ADB). (3) Sami Khan, a daily wage laborer, waited on Murree road's roadside during the COVID-19 lockdown in Pakistan (photo by Rahim Mirza/ADB). (4) A Sri Lankan Muslim shop keeper arranges sweets prior to Ramadan celebration in Colombo, Sri Lanka. Muslims around the world are preparing to celebrate Eid al-Fitr, the three-day festival marking the end of the Muslim holy fasting month but the government imposed an island-wide curfew due to the corona virus pandemic (photo by M.A. Pushpa Kumara). (5) Training facilitators from Vena Energy, Mataram University, and the local government helped the women of Jeger Buana Lombok to expand their market for their cassava chips business (photo by Achmad Ibrahim/ADB).

Cover design by Anthony Villanueva.

Contents

Tables and Figures

Figures

Acknowledgments

This Guidance Note, *COVID-19 and the Finance Sector in Asia and the Pacific*, was prepared by the Finance Sector Group (FSG) under the Sustainable Development and Climate Change Department (SDCC) of the Asian Development Bank (ADB). This is part of a series of ADB guidance notes produced in response to the coronavirus disease (COVID-19) pandemic.

Junkyu Lee, chief of FSG, SDCC, led production of the note, with a key contribution from Thomas Kessler, principal finance sector specialist (disaster insurance). Valuable technical inputs and comments were provided by FSG secretariat team colleagues, in particular; Arup Kumar, principal finance sector specialist; Sung Su Kim, finance sector specialist (inclusive finance); Hyungchan Lee, finance sector specialist (capital markets); Lisette Cipriano, senior digital technology specialist (financial technology services); Jae Deuk Lee, finance sector specialist; Raquel R. Borres, senior economic officer; and with support from Katherine Mitzi Ho. Co, associate operations analyst; and Matilde Mila D. Cauinian, operations assistant.

The team also appreciates the guidance from ADB's FSG committee co-chaired by Christine Engstrom, director, Private Sector Operations Department; and Tariq Niazi, director, Central and West Asia Department along with the members: Xiaoqin Fan, director, East Asia Department; Lotte Schou-Zibell, regional director, Pacific Department; Sabyasachi Mitra, director, South Asia Department; Jose Antonio Tan, director, Southeast Asia Department; Satoru Yamadera, advisor, Economics Research and Regional Cooperation Department; and Jonathan Grosvenor, assistant treasurer, Treasury Department. Likewise, it has valued the support and advice of the operations departments, in particular, Irfan A. Qureshi, Jennifer Romero-Torres, Aziz Haydarov, Giacomo Giuseppe, and Shiu Raj Singh.

The FSG Secretariat team greatly appreciates SDCC Director General Bruno Carrasco's overall direction on the post-COVID-19 financial policy considerations. SDCC Chief Sector Officer Robert Guild provided guidance on preparation of the publication to enhance quality and structure, with encouragement for FSG secretariat colleagues.

The team is grateful for substantial research contributions from ADB consultants Mikko Marl V. Diaz and Alyssa Villanueva. Editing consultant to FSG, Eric Van Zant, edited the file.

Abbreviations

ADB	Asian Development Bank
ASEAN	Association of Southeast Asian Nations
bps	basis points
COVID-19	coronavirus disease
DMC	developing member country
ERIA	Economic Research Institute for ASEAN and East Asia
FSG	Finance Sector Group
GDP	gross domestic product
ILO	International Labour Organization
IMF	International Monetary Fund
KYC	know-your-customer
MSME	micro, small, and medium-sized enterprises
NPL	nonperforming loan
OECD	Organisation for Economic Co-operation and Development
SDCC	Sustainable Development and Climate Change Department
SME	small and medium-sized enterprises
UN	United Nations
VAT	value-added tax

Executive Summary: Key Messages

The coronavirus disease (COVID-19) economic crisis, unlike the global financial crisis over a decade ago, did not arise in the finance sector. Indeed, finance was generally healthy globally before the pandemic emerged. As the crisis broke, there was a need for urgent liquidity, but concern was not immediate that this was evolving into an insolvency crisis.

However, the emergency measures taken to contain the ongoing health crisis have had severe impacts on some of the most vulnerable sectors of real economies as lockdowns have interrupted businesses across countries. The liquidity crisis thus began to translate into growing insolvencies, and this impact continues as countries struggle to develop and distribute effective vaccines fast enough. The concentrated risk for real economies has thus been unremitting in many countries, eventually with negative impact on their financial sectors.

Additionally, although the economic impacts from the two global crises—2008 and 2020—have different origins, they are similar in some ways. Navigation of the recovery in economies and finance sectors calls for adept policy thinking that can avoid a "new normal 2.0", a sequel to the "new normal 1.0" in the wake of the global financial crisis over a decade ago. Likewise, economic thinkers are cautioning again that policy makers need to avoid falling into complacency as the crisis evolves.

This report therefore closely examines the effects of the pandemic on real economies. It looks at the transmission of these effects into finance sectors and the many measures taken to ease the impact. It also examines the harmful impact on three crucial elements in the Asia and Pacific economies—migrant workers and remittances, the small enterprises that are their economic backbone, and banking—and the threat these hold for financial stability, including through an anticipated rise in nonperforming assets. It then reviews a series of measures that can mitigate pressures on people, businesses, and finance sectors—including broader use of such things as social security protection, modern insurance products, and greater digitization in the finance sector.

These options can help authorities adapt effectively through the rapid changes of the unfolding pandemic and better prepare for future pandemics.

The following summarizes key messages in the report.

Real Impact on People, Small Businesses, and the Broader Economy

- *Economies and labor markets contracted across Asia and the Pacific:* COVID-19 hit the poor and vulnerable hard, particularly informal workers. Estimates suggest that the second quarter 2020 working hours dropped 13.5% in the region, equivalent to 235 million full-time jobs.

- *Initially, remittances declined to some Asian markets.* April 2020 saw major declines in nearly every market. In March 2020, the World Bank predicted that global remittance flows would decline by 20% (World Bank 2020c). The prediction has since been revised to a fall of 7%, to $508 billion in 2020 (World Bank 2020a.)
- *Small businesses took the brunt of the reduction in global demand for products and services.* This slashed employment across the region, compounding the difficulties such firms already faced in accessing finance.
- *Banking sector assets are expected to deteriorate as loans turn bad.* Nonperforming loans are expected to rise and require attention in the near term. The sector has faced liquidity stress from global financing markets and credit losses on companies and households.
- *Crisis impacts are in turn creating turbulence in financial markets, regionally and globally.* The combined effects of economic losses, decreasing market confidence, and social-distancing measures to contain the virus spread have at points led to financial market turmoil far worse than in 2008–2009.
- *All of this has slashed economic growth.* The Asian Development Bank (ADB) reported negative gross domestic product growth of –0.1% in developing Asia in 2020, with contractions in all regions except for East Asia.

Policy Responses and Considerations

Short-term responses

- *Unprecedented fiscal, monetary, and emergency liquidity support to maintain financial stability.* Lessons from previous crises have informed the role of immediate and effective policy response in maintaining financial stability. Policymakers have implemented a slew of accommodative monetary and financial policies to ease financial stress and liquidity and help absorb shocks to the financial system. These include policy rate cuts and temporary relaxation of macroprudential tools and regulatory forbearance.
- *Limited mobility and work-from-home arrangements forced rapid adoption of digital financial services.* Rapid digitization of the finance sector has not only helped economies in containing the spread of the virus, but also helped governments disburse financial assistance quickly and effectively. It enabled firms and households to rapidly access online payments and financing. Additionally, digitization has helped in ensuring business continuity and survival as well as increasing financial inclusion, especially for micro, small, and medium-sized enterprises (MSMEs).
- *Assisting households through coordinated social protection, aggressive labor market policies, and job creation programs.* The most common interventions have been cash transfers, special social allowances and grants, followed by income and jobs protection. In some countries, social protection schemes, like unemployment insurance, combined with cash distributions to low- and middle-income groups, ensured continued household spending, safeguarded retail borrowers' credit quality, and operated as social, economic, and financial stabilizers to allow quicker recovery.
- *Assisting remittance-reliant households through favorable remittance policies and employment support measures.* Source and home countries globally have cooperated in addressing the issues of declining remittances. A number of countries alongside international organizations have committed to a call to action and have implemented regulations to aid the remittance industry. Source countries implemented employment retention policies for laid-off migrant workers, while home countries eased tax regulations and transaction fees for inward remittances.
- *Supporting MSMEs to preserve employment and their quick recovery.* Small and medium-sized enterprise (SME) assistance has been a major focus of urgent government stimulus programs. Measures include moratorium on principal and interest repayments to restructuring of loans, employment assistance and tax relief to ease financial difficulties and liquidity issues. Other actions include low interest loans, enhanced

credit insurance, credit guarantees to banks, regulatory forbearance, and accelerated digitalization to stimulate lending to MSMEs.

- *Banking and capital markets.* Common features implemented across Asia included increasing the liquidity of banking institutions and the capital market, through the following measures: (i) policy interest rate cuts, (ii) deregulation of reserve requirement ratios and other regulatory ratios for financial institutions, (iii) central bank liquidity injections, (iv) regulatory forbearance to free up bank liquidity, (v) broadening eligible collateral for repo transactions as liquidity support, and (vi) outright purchases of government bonds and corporate bonds and securities.
- *Insurance and pensions.* Important measures included ensuring grace period for payment of insurance premiums, deferred payment or temporary reduction in premium contributions, and timely settlement of claims to maintain public confidence in the insurance industry. Insurance companies began popularizing health insurance, providing lines of credit to MSMEs, and support for insurance agents and intermediaries to continue servicing their customers. Forbearance policies aimed at capital preservation, improved risk management and reporting were also announced. They helped insurers remain resilient and continue to underwrite risk on their books.

Medium-term policy considerations

- *Establishing a financial framework for epidemic risk financing to identify critical risks and financing gaps to national emergency, health, and fiscal systems.* This framework can help fill financial and technical shortcomings exposed during the crisis due to the lack of or timely availability of national funds and financial instruments. In addition, it can bolster governments' financial resilience by complementing existing regional financial safety nets and enabling access to emergency funds on time-based, predefined criteria and payout thresholds. Crowding in the private sector can help explore a diverse range of risk financing tools like insurance, reinsurance, and insurance-linked securities to also support affected economic sectors, such as MSMEs and most vulnerable populations. It will thus facilitate response in all aspects of the crisis and containing epidemic outbreaks before they assume pandemic proportions.
- *Buttressing financial stability and macroprudential policies.* While the immediate policy responses implemented worldwide have effectively mitigated the health crisis and maintained financial markets, these have enabled the buildup of financial imbalances and vulnerabilities such as unsustainable debt and reduced credit quality. These would likely cause damage to long-term financial stability and financial development. Alongside this issue, the ongoing pandemic challenges, including virus mutations and divergent economic growth across the developed and developing economies, continue to pose risks with high uncertainties. Therefore, policymakers should seek to implement policies that balance financial stability and growth under the context of major increases in public debt and potential nonperforming loans. A well-designed, communicated, and measured exit strategy is also needed to ensure a sustained economic recovery and financial stability.
- *Developing insurance markets for risk sharing and transfer solutions.* COVID-19 has harmed Asia's insurance and pensions sector. For insurers, the pandemic response has significant financial ramifications, including income uncertainty due to reduced or delayed renewals and a reduction in new business, higher claim frequency and severity, capital impacts, and altered risk profiles and business mixes. The withdrawal of forbearance measures should be orderly, well sequenced, and coordinated. It must be based on proper analysis

of risks to ensure that they remain resilient and continue to underwrite risk and introduce innovative products but also enjoy public trust.

- **Improving SME financing for Asia's developing countries.** Policymakers should explore new financing options, hitherto less utilized or unutilized, for MSMEs such as credit guarantee/insurance and innovative technologies to fill in gaps in financial security and providing coverage for lost income resulting from economic disruptions. During the pandemic, relief was meant to ensure business continuity, preserve jobs, and provide sufficient money for functioning businesses, as well as aid MSMEs in their recovery. Accommodative macroeconomic and financial policies have helped MSMEs access to banks and nonbank financial institutions. This should be further complemented with private sector support that is well-targeted to provide vital financial relief to MSMEs. Multilateral banks can help SMEs by promoting and creating best practices in small business finance, credit guarantee schemes, and credit insurance.

- **Fostering digital transformation in the finance sector.** The pandemic has challenged financial institutions to provide more effective and convenient digital solutions for payments and financial services amid the lockdown measures and physical distancing. To foster digital transformation in the finance sector, policymakers must promote appropriate digital financial frameworks and actions to support data connectivity, mobile technology, digital banking, and fintech. These will encourage contactless and cashless transactions while promoting financial inclusion as digitization makes financial services more accessible to underserved and unbanked communities. This is especially vital for large informal sectors in emerging Asia. Yet, smooth transition to digital financial services must also need sufficient digital infrastructure for access to the internet and mobile connectivity. The demand for digital financial services has increased the need for a commensurate scale-up of know-your-customer and anti-money laundering and countering financing of terrorist regulations. Therefore, policies must respond to new challenges such as cybercrime and digital fraud, brought by vulnerabilities in the rapid expansion of digitization. Policymakers need to strengthen supervision and regulation to ensure financial stability and a safe fintech environment for consumers and investors.

1 Introduction

More than a year since the outbreak of coronavirus disease (COVID-19), governments around the world have implemented measures and strategies to cope with the economic and financial impacts. But if policymakers are to continue to ably respond as the pandemic rapidly evolves, particularly as vaccine strategies emerge, they need to take stock of what has passed and explore measures for improvement.

Indeed, navigation of the recovery in economies and finance sectors calls for adept policy thinking that can avoid a "new normal 2.0," a sequel to the original new normal in the wake of the global financial crisis over a decade ago.[1] Then, economic thinkers sounded an alarm about complacency in policy responses that, if uncorrected, would bar a return to the high growth and low inflation before 2008.

In 2008 and in 2020, initial responses impressively warded off much worse calamity. But now, as then, the measures employed entail costs and risks that call for careful and sustained policy action that adapts as the economic and financial effects of the crisis and the responses evolve. Such action can avoid "lower productivity, higher debt, and more sluggish demand" due to COVID-19 shock, which could unleash "even lower growth and higher financial instability" (Mayeda 2020).

It is in this context that this note aims to serve a role. The note is not an "alert" to finance sector players of a string of new policy options already in the dock. Rather, it is a stocktaking of where finance sectors are now, a year into the pandemic and measures that could prove useful to decision makers as they navigate fast-evolving financial waters.

Few can be unaware of the severe disruptions to the global economy unleashed as countries around the world quickly implemented lockdowns to contain the virus. Restrictions on movement and social distancing measures have badly hurt real sectors (e.g., tourism, manufacturing, transportation, and other services) and global business disruptions are felt in the banking industry and the overall finance sector.

---

[1] El-Erian (2009) characterized the post-global financial crisis *new normal* as a period of low growth and high unemployment. There was a warning that the impact of the COVID-19 pandemic could lead to a worse *new normal 2.0* characterized by lower growth, higher inequality, and more tenuous financial stability.

Governments responded quickly with decisive policy action and timely liquidity injections that have alleviated concerns in targeted sectors of the real economy. However, some policy measures have enabled a lack of transparency in reporting standards and other practices among businesses, if only temporarily, and have held back needed reforms. This could eventually lead to bigger challenges for the stability of the finance sector and its development in the long run.

Conditions of the finance sector in many developing member countries in this region were already weak as a mysterious flu-like illness first gained attention in late 2019 and into 2020, and they worsened as the crisis unfolded. Across the region, for example, nonperforming loans (NPLs) had already been rising among banking and nonbanking institutions as lockdown measures hit small business and household financial capacity. Additionally, countries faced a severe lack of capital market liquidity after international investors flocked to safe-haven assets amid tighter global conditions as the crisis broke.

Policies designed to rescue real sectors may thus weaken financial system foundations with high and unsustainable debt and rising NPLs post-crisis unless proper resolution policy frameworks and measures are in place. Countries with thin capital buffers in their banking sectors will have to deal with the anticipated rise in NPLs in the near term, before it becomes unmanageable.

Policy makers should also implement measures that can bring about a sustainable, resilient, and quick economic and finance sector recovery after COVID-19. Indeed, doing so requires a new normal, one that provides a system with well-balanced allocation of resources and constant monitoring and managing of the known and newly emerging risks in the finance sector, including cyber risks and environmental, social, and governance risks. Public and private cooperation will be central to economic recovery and will require a coordinated approach that balances finance sector development with an enabling regulatory and supervisory environment.

A key element in this new normal in the finance sector is the rapid digitization of financial infrastructure and services. The debilitating impacts of COVID-19 notwithstanding, the pandemic has also accelerated the transition toward digitization of finance. Many governments have experienced and recognized the importance of digitized social infrastructure, including financial infrastructure, for tackling the spread of disease as well as for securing business continuity and pandemic resilience. Digital acceleration will be at the forefront of every financial institution and business post crisis. In supporting this trend, regulators and policy makers must ensure equitable access and privacy for all.

The paper explores the problems and the solutions laid bare by the pandemic. Section II summarizes initial pandemic impact on individuals; micro, small and medium-sized enterprises; the banking and capital sectors; and the broader finance sector. Section III reviews immediate government responses to address the issues in selected sectors. Section IV provides medium-term policy considerations for recovery and finance sector development post-COVID-19, identifying a series of challenges and issues that have emerged and measures that can be used to solve them. The last section concludes with several key takeaways.

2 Finance Sector Impacts of COVID-19

Uncertainties at the onset of the COVID-19 pandemic led to a short-lived but significant disruption in global financial markets characterized by volatility in capital markets and large capital outflows from emerging markets. While global financial markets have managed the negative impacts of the pandemic relatively well so far, the ensuing health crisis and efforts to control its spread could lead to adverse long-term impact in the real sector.

These containment and social distancing policies have caused prolonged interruptions and even business closures in select industries—travel and hospitality, food services, and wholesale and retail trade—all areas where micro, small, and medium-sized enterprises (MSMEs) are prominent. This has affected the household level, as business interruptions have caused massive labor shocks, leading to loss in working-hours and even prolonged unemployment for more vulnerable populations. Together, this disruption in the real sector threatens asset quality of banks and endangers long-term financial stability.

Households' Vulnerabilities to Shocks

The economic fallout of the COVID-19 pandemic resulted in a significant labor shock as unemployment and underemployment surged, hitting women and young people especially hard. As of June 2020, about 93% of the world's workers resided in countries with workplace closures of some kind still in force, according to the International Labour Organization (ILO). Global working-hours declined an estimated 14% in the second quarter of 2020 (equivalent to 400 million full-time jobs) over the last quarter of 2019 due to these measures. In Asia and the Pacific, total working hours in the second quarter dropped an estimated 13.5% (equivalent to 235 million full-time jobs) (ILO 2020a).

The impact on women has been much more pronounced, as they are more exposed to hard-hit sectors. According to a study by United Nations (UN) Women and the United Nations Development Programme, an additional 47 million women will be pushed below the poverty line ($1.90/day) as a result of the COVID-19 pandemic (UN Women 2020). Similarly, the pandemic has heavily disrupted employment conditions and prospects for young workers (aged 18–24). An ILO study in 2020 indicates that 17% of young workers employed before the outbreak had stopped working and that working hours for the youth had dropped an average of 2 hours per day (ILO 2020b).

Such closures likely impacted the poor hardest, most of whom work in informal sectors that lack access to health care and social protection. ILO estimated that income losses would be substantial, with almost 1.6 billion informal workers (76% of global informal employment) significantly affected by lockdown measures; the loss in income potential is anticipated to increase relative poverty for informal workers by 34 percentage points globally (ILO 2020b).[2] ILO estimates that 1.3 billion people (68.2% of the employed) in Asia and the Pacific make their living in the informal economy; Table 1 presents numbers for select Asian countries. Despite a vast range of fiscal and financial measures implemented for workers—subsidies, grants, and financial benefits—many remain exposed to additional risks and vulnerabilities. For example, in Asia, governments have limited policies that can effectively reach the informal sector (ILO 2020c).

Table 1: Informal Employment
(% of total nonagricultural employment)

Economy	Informal Employment	Year
Bangladesh	91.30	2017
Cambodia	90.56	2012
India	80.28	2018
Nepal	77.62	2017
Indonesia	76.47	2018
Lao PDR	75.50	2017
Pakistan	71.23	2018
Sri Lanka	65.93	2016
Viet Nam	54.90	2018
Timor-Leste	53.70	2013
Thailand	51.42	2018
Brunei Darussalam	32.36	2017
Mongolia	30.93	2018
Armenia	24.75	2017

Lao PDR = Lao People's Democratic Republic.

Source: Index Mundi.

The income and labor effects of the crisis on the vulnerable population (blue-collar workers that work in affected sectors) will severely affect global poverty and income inequality. The Poverty and Shared Prosperity Report 2020 (World Bank 2020b) reported that the economic impact of COVID-19 including job loss and reduced earnings likely pushed between 88 and 115 million people into extreme poverty (income under $1.90/day) in 2020. Additionally, a study by Furceri et al. (2020) indicates that policies undertaken to combat previous pandemics have raised income inequality. During the COVID-19 pandemic, countries have allotted

2 Relative poverty is defined as the proportion of workers with monthly earnings below 50% of median earnings in the population.

fiscal programs to stabilize their automotive and aviation companies, but many programs lack access and reach to the most vulnerable households.

The threat of reduced working hours and outright unemployment has also put loan repayments and overall financial stability at risk. Global household debt stood around $40 trillion at the end of 2019—$14 trillion of which came from major economies in Asia (Table 2)—and banks' claims on the household sector represented 20%–40% of their total asset portfolio (Zabai 2020).

Table 2: Total Credit to Households in Selected Asian Economies, Fourth Quarter 2019

Economy	Total GDP ($ billion)	Total Credit to Households ($ billion)	Total Credit to Households (% of GDP)
China, People's Republic of	14,217	7,848	55.2
Hong Kong, China	368	297	80.7
India	2,795	341	12.2
Indonesia	1,141	194	17.0
Japan	5,102	3,015	59.1
Korea, Republic of	1,658	1,583	95.5
Malaysia	370	252	68.2
Singapore	376	195	51.8
Thailand	568	393	69.2
Total	**26,595**	**14,118**	**53.1**

GDP = gross domestic product.

Source: Bank for International Settlements. Bank Statistics Explorer. https://stats.bis.org/statx/toc/CRE.html (accessed 5 July 2020).

Households with little liquidity buffer and that fall below yearly subsistence levels are less likely to be financially resilient against the employment shocks of the COVID-19 pandemic (Zabai 2020). Zabai estimates that "household resilience" for the bottom 20% of people in Organisation for Economic Co-operation and Development (OECD) countries covers less than 3 months.[3] Microfinance institutions, which cater mostly to low-income households, face existential threats, as they require high repayment rates to be sustainable. Because their customers' incomes remain constrained, repayment rates are expected to fall (Consultative Group to Assist the Poorest 2020). Surveys in Cambodia, Indonesia, and Nepal indicate that microfinance institutions have significant liquidity shortfalls and urgently need liquidity.

---

[3] Household resilience is defined as the number of periods (months or years) during which a household can cover subsistence consumption and debt service with liquid assets in case of income loss.

Remittances

Remittances are a substantial source of external funding and a large share of gross domestic product (GDP) for many Asian countries. On average, remittance inflows into Asia have been about 10 times the level of official development assistance since 2012. In 2019, by GDP share, four of the top-five remittance receiving countries were in Asia and the Pacific: Tonga (37.16%), Tajikistan (27.97%), the Kyrgyz Republic (27.17), and Nepal (24.12%) (Figure 1).[4]

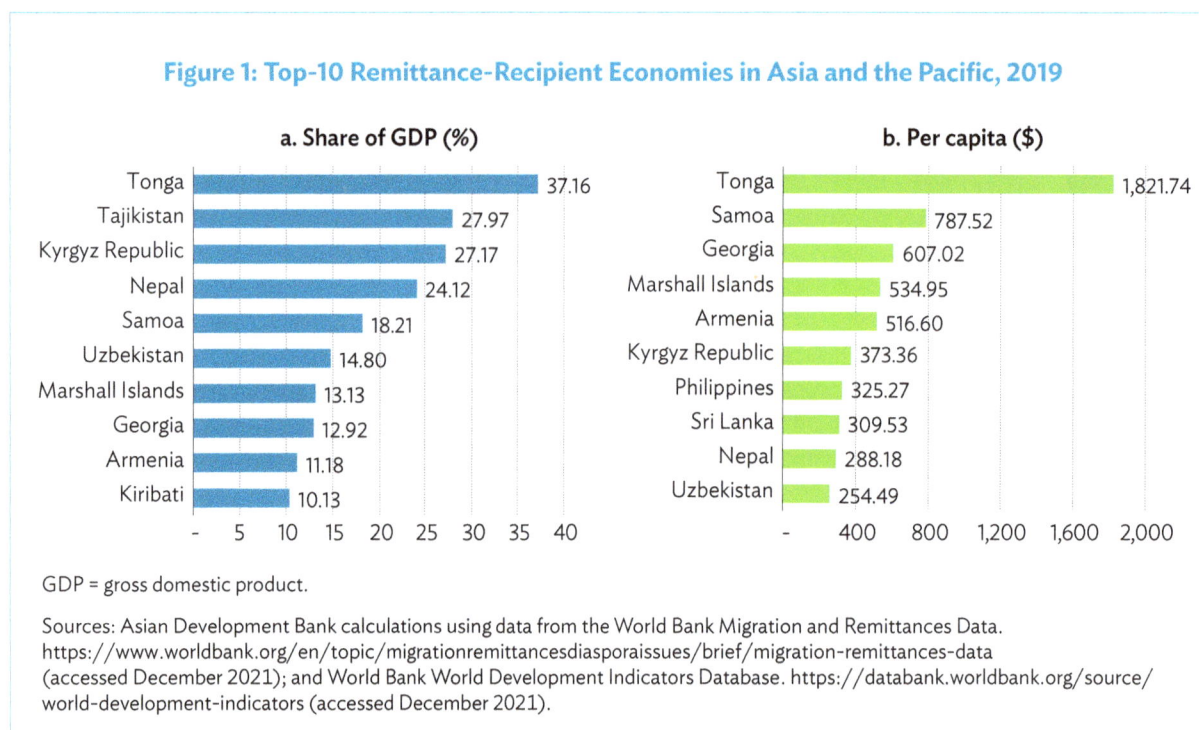

Figure 1: Top-10 Remittance-Recipient Economies in Asia and the Pacific, 2019

a. Share of GDP (%)

Economy	%
Tonga	37.16
Tajikistan	27.97
Kyrgyz Republic	27.17
Nepal	24.12
Samoa	18.21
Uzbekistan	14.80
Marshall Islands	13.13
Georgia	12.92
Armenia	11.18
Kiribati	10.13

b. Per capita ($)

Economy	$
Tonga	1,821.74
Samoa	787.52
Georgia	607.02
Marshall Islands	534.95
Armenia	516.60
Kyrgyz Republic	373.36
Philippines	325.27
Sri Lanka	309.53
Nepal	288.18
Uzbekistan	254.49

GDP = gross domestic product.

Sources: Asian Development Bank calculations using data from the World Bank Migration and Remittances Data. https://www.worldbank.org/en/topic/migrationremittancesdiasporaissues/brief/migration-remittances-data (accessed December 2021); and World Bank World Development Indicators Database. https://databank.worldbank.org/source/world-development-indicators (accessed December 2021).

Containment measures implemented to control COVID-19 have greatly disrupted economic activity, including the remittance industry. The Asian Development Bank (ADB) reported negative GDP growth of -0.1% in developing Asia in 2020, with contractions in all regions except for East Asia (ADB 2021). The crisis hit the top remittance recipient economies in the region severely at the height of the pandemic, and migrant workers have found themselves unemployed and forced to return home with low prospects of returning to work immediately. About 91 million international migrants from Asia and the Pacific were vulnerable to the economic effects of the pandemic (Takenaka et al. 2020). In Tajikistan, an estimated 500,000 migrant workers (5.2% of the population) were unable to return to as the pandemic hit the Russian Federation (ADB 2020a). In the Philippines, the fourth-largest remittance receiving country by volume in the world, thousands of overseas Filipino workers returned home and 300,000 more were expected to arrive in the 3 months through June 2020 (Parrocha 2020).

---

[4] World Bank. Migration and Remittances Data. https://www.worldbank.org/en/topic/migrationremittancesdiasporaissues/brief/migration-remittances-data (accessed March 2021).

Declining remittance inflows have also put household finances and financial systems at risk. ADB studies have found that the disruption of remittance flows severely affects remittance-dependent households and could raise poverty and create challenges in meeting basic expenditures such as education, health, and loan repayments (Takenaka et al. 2020).

Additionally, Barajas et al. (2018) illustrate that at a high level of remittances-to-GDP, deposits grow as remittance flows increase. The increase in deposits allows banks to increase financial services to the private sector. Aggarwal, Demirgüç-Kunt, and Martínez Pería (2011) show that remittances are significantly and positively correlated with deposit- and credit-to-GDP ratios. Capacity of banks to extend credit will be greatly reduced as these sources of funding are lost and amid higher interest rates brought about by government measures.

Because primary remittance source economies have slowed, a large decline in remittances is unavoidable. For example, the World Bank estimates that, globally, remittances would decline 7.2% in 2020 (World Bank 2020a; Yap and Alfredo 2020). The declines in 2020 and 2021 will affect all regions, with the steepest drop expected in Europe and Central Asia (by 16% and 8%, respectively), followed by East Asia and the Pacific (11% and 4%), and South Asia (4%).

Initially, as the viral outbreak continued, remittances to some Asian markets declined, with major declines in nearly every market in April 2020. Bangladesh fell 25%, Sri Lanka fell 14%, and the Philippines fell 16% year-on-year for that month (World Bank 2020a). However, from June 2020, some countries started to show signs of recovery. Bangladesh (18.6%), Fiji (8.7%), Georgia (8.8%), and Pakistan (17.4%) all received higher remittances in 2020 compared to 2019 (Figure 2). Despite the slowdown of the global economy, remittances from migrant workers managed to stay afloat due to the expansion of social assistance programs and unemployment insurance in more developed economies (Takenaka, Kim, and Gaspar 2020). Despite resilience in the remittances industry, policy makers should remain wary of a resurgence of economic restrictions, especially as global cases of the COVID-19 virus have picked up since February 2021.

Figure 2: Changes in Remittance Receipts, Selected Asia and Pacific Countries,
Comparable Periods in 2019, 2020
(%)

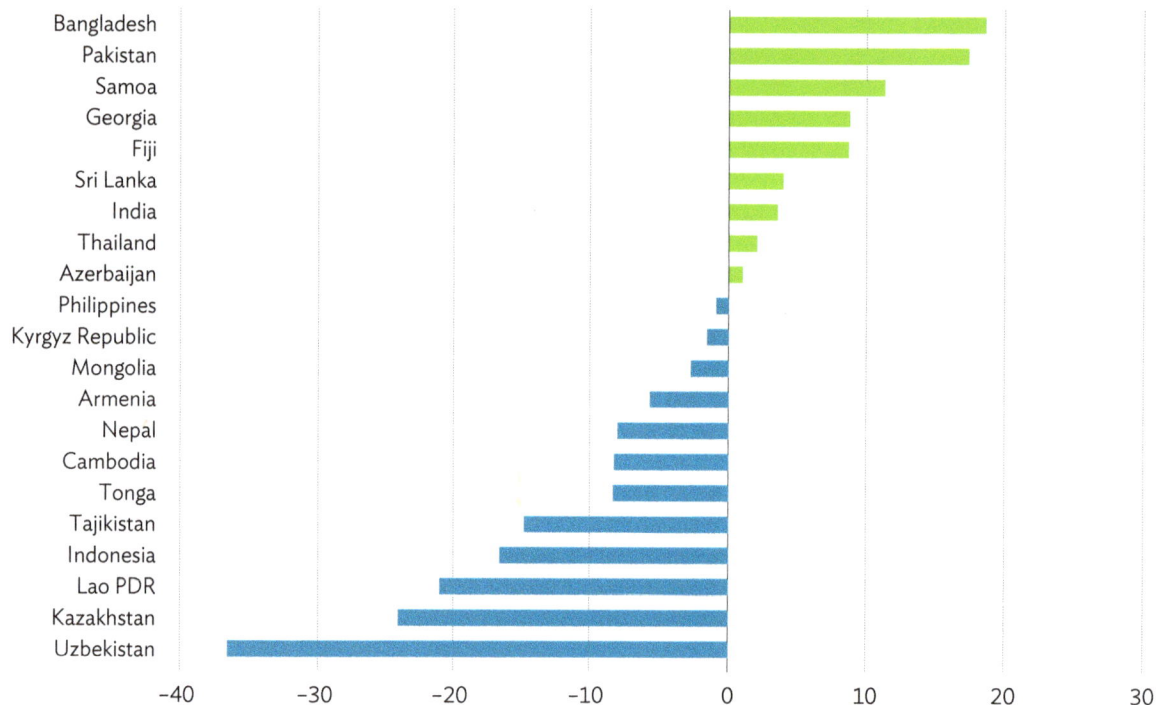

Lao PDR = Lao People's Democratic Republic.

Note: Remittance data for Bangladesh, Fiji, Georgia, and Pakistan refer to January to December; data for Armenia, Kazakhstan, the Kyrgyz Republic, the Philippines, Samoa, and Sri Lanka are from January to November; Azerbaijan, Cambodia, India, the Lao PDR, Mongolia, Nepal, Tajikistan, Thailand, Tonga, and Uzbekistan are first-half year's data; and Indonesia data refers to the first three quarters.

Source: Takenaka, A., K. Kim, and R. Gaspar. 2020. Despite the Pandemic, Remittances Have Kept Flowing Home to Asia's Families. *Asian Development Blog*. https://blogs.adb.org/blog/despite-pandemic-remittances-have-kept-flowing-home-asia-s-families.

Micro, Small, and Medium-Sized Enterprises

Micro, small, and medium-sized enterprises (MSMEs) play a major role in most economies, particularly developing economies. According to the World Bank, formal small and medium-sized enterprises (SMEs) contributed up to 40% of GDP in emerging economies and represented about 90% of businesses and more than 50% of worldwide employment (World Bank n.d.). This is especially true in Asia, given the importance of MSMEs in the region to the global economy. According to the Asia SME Finance Monitor 2020 (ADB 2020b), from 2010–2019, SMEs accounted for 97% of all enterprises, 69% of employment, and an average of 41% of GDP in Southeast Asia (ADB 2020b).

It is therefore a significant concern that the MSME sector has taken the brunt of the reduction in global demand for its products and services as demand from global value chains has declined and restrictions on movement of consumers have remained in place in many countries. The hardest-hit sectors include travel and hospitality, food services, and wholesale and retail trade, which have big MSME representation (Economic Research Institute for ASEAN and East Asia [ERIA] 2020a). Own-account workers and small enterprises together account for more than 70% of global employment in retail trade and nearly 60% in the accommodation and food services sector (ILO 2020b). Factories have ceased production, bricks-and-mortar retail stores and restaurants have closed, commodity prices have plunged, and overseas and domestic travel have been curtailed (Congressional Research Service 2020).

Travel restrictions have had severe impact on the tourism industry—especially in Asian and Pacific economies that heavily depend on tourism receipts (Figure 3). The real economic impact is large, with the World Travel and Tourism Council estimating that the pandemic will ultimately lead to a loss of more than 60 million jobs in the travel and tourism industry in Asia and the Pacific. Confounding these issues are subdued recovery of the tourism industry, with willingness to travel—as represented by bookings for future travel—down 70% year-on-year in January 2021. The emergence of potentially more infectious virus strains and slower than expected rollout of vaccination in many locations is not helping (International Air Transport Association 2020).

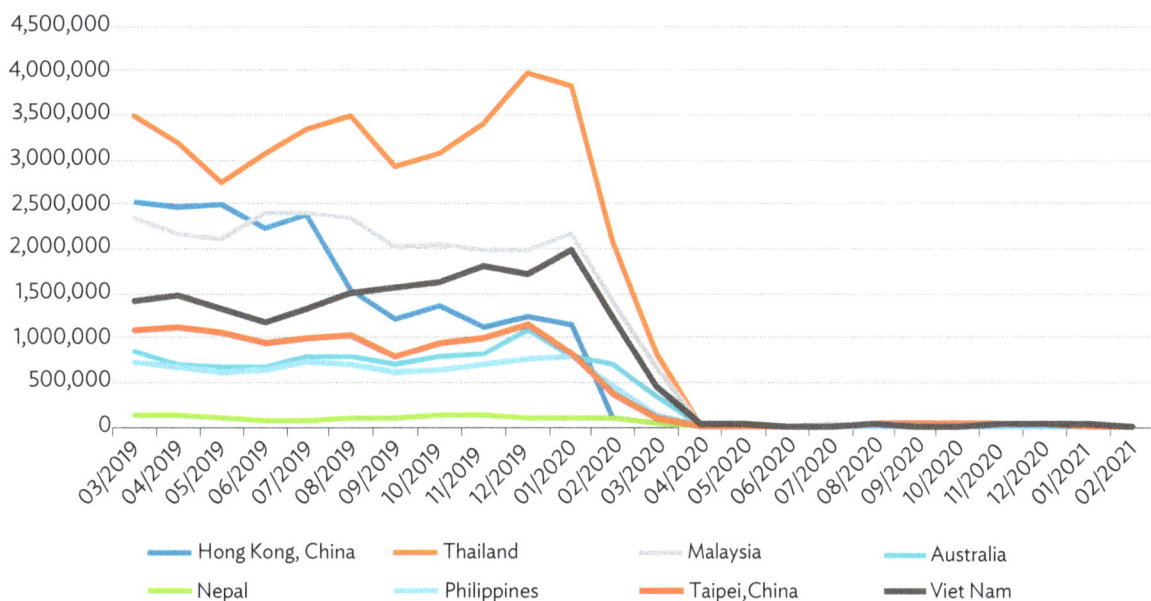

Figure 3: Monthly Tourist Arrivals in Selected Asian Economies

GDP = gross domestic product.

Note: Only Asian economies with major tourism industries (> 2.5% of GDP) and with complete data during March 2019 to December 2020 were included.

Source: CEIC data. https://insights.ceicdata.com/ (accessed 20 April 2021).

These containment measures have also affected agriculture sectors through restrictions on domestic and international movement of food and agricultural products. This has severely undermined incomes of farmers, agricultural SMEs, and food security among households. An ADB study reported that lockdown measures implemented by Pakistan have disrupted production and trade of highly perishable goods, such as fruits, vegetables, and dairy.[5]

According to the OECD, MSME vulnerabilities arise through both supply and demand channels:

Supply channel

- Loss of labor: Companies could see the supply of labor fall as workers fall ill or need to look after children or other dependents with schools closed. The ILO estimated in 2020 that COVID-19 responses could see global unemployment reach 5.3 million (low scenario) and 24.7 million (high scenario) as movements of people are restricted. Lockdowns and quarantines also lead to further and more severe drops in capacity utilization.

- Supply chains: SMEs relying on suppliers from other countries and regions become more vulnerable due to obstacles in transportation by road, sea, and air imposed by containment and mitigation. In a Tokyo Shoko Research survey on the effects of the outbreak on firms, consisting mainly of SMEs, 39% of respondents reported supply-chain disruptions alongside a 26% decrease in sales orders (Tokyo Shoko Research 2020).

Demand channel

- Reduced demand and SME credits: Businesses, including SMEs, will bear the brunt of lower global demand for their products and services (OECD 2020b). Large and sudden loss of demand and revenue for SMEs can strongly curtail ability to function or cause severe liquidity shortages and balance sheet deterioration. Bank and nonbank financial institutions are therefore likely reluctant to provide the needed credit to SMEs with restricted access to capital markets.

- Further, consumers may lose income, continue to fear contagion, and suffer considerable uncertainty, and in turn reduce spending and consumption. Layoffs and firms unable to pay salaries compound these effects.

- Restrictions on movement and social distancing: SMEs in tourism, transportation, restaurants, and retail and wholesale trade have likely felt the effect more significantly. OECD estimates these industries stood to lose around 50%–100% in consumer spending (OECD 2020b).

Given the limited resources of SMEs, these firms are less resilient and flexible in dealing with pandemic costs. The International Finance Corporation estimates that 65 million firms, 40% of formal MSMEs in developing countries, have unmet financing needs of $5.2 trillion every year (World Bank n.d.). The Asia SME Finance Monitor 2020 (ADB 2020b) reports that the MSME credit market in Southeast Asia is small but growing—with bank loans to MSMEs averaging 14.8% of countries' GDP and 16.9% of total bank lending during 2010–2019, contracting at a compound annual rate of 1.3% and 0.3%, respectively. Additionally, while nonbank financial institutions remain viable alternatives to bank financing, these institutions do not target MSMEs as borrowers.

Yoshino and Taghizadeh-Hesary (2018) highlight that Asian SMEs have difficulty accessing cheap financing, as banks prefer lending to larger enterprises with more transparent accounting practices. In addition, other literature points to issues of asymmetric information (between the borrower and lender), which note that SMEs find it challenging to produce financial records and coherent business plans, severely limiting their access to traditional financing networks (Berger and Udell 2005).

---

[5] ADB. 2020. *COVID-19 Impact on Farm Households in Punjab, Pakistan: Analysis of Data from a Cross-Sectional Survey*. Manila.

The issues hampering SME access to finance before the pandemic—arising from low business activity and including failure to pay wages, rent, loan repayments, and other financial obligations—now exacerbate their financial difficulties. Unlike larger firms, otherwise solvent SMEs face an immediate risk of bankruptcy while containment and mitigation measures are still in force (OECD 2020b). In the People's Republic of China, for example, more than 460,000 firms closed permanently—mostly SMEs—in the first quarter of 2020 (Leng 2020).

Banking Sector

The experience of the 2008 global financial crisis left the banks to deal with the post-crisis market climate and modifications to existing regulatory frameworks. A new banking operating landscape has been adopted, concentrating on improved global prudential framework and supervision reforms. Through the new financial regulatory framework to transform the global financial system including Basel III's stronger capital and liquidity buffers, these finance sector reforms have strengthened banks' resilience while reducing implicit state subsidies and the impact of bank failure on the economy (Bank for International Settlements 2018). Today, more than a decade after the global financial crisis shook the world's banking system, another crisis threatens to wreak havoc. Insolvency issues have not occurred due to the impacts of the COVID-19 pandemic, but liquidity problems have resulted from the pandemic's demand and supply shocks. Despite this, the finance sector remained resilient as banks are better capitalized and have less exposure to liquidity and funding risks, thanks to post-global financial crisis bank restructuring efforts underpinned by strong foundations.

Global disruptions in business activity caused by the ongoing pandemic are putting pressure on banking performance amid liquidity stress from global financing markets and credit losses on companies and households. The businesses that can be severely affected by restrictions on movement and social distancing—such as tourism, transportation, restaurants, and retail and wholesale trade, as noted—face a high risk of default as slowing business will severely undermine their debt servicing capacity. Banks and nonbank financial institutions face continuously deteriorating credit quality as factories cease production, retail stores and restaurants close, and overseas and domestic travel shrink (Congressional Research Service 2020). These difficulties are translated to households as banks are indirectly exposed to deteriorating household credit as unemployment rises in the vulnerable business sectors.

Confounding this issue was the severe liquidity stress caused by extreme demand for liquid assets that impaired activity in usually highly liquid funding markets. The market strain forced policy makers across the globe to adopt large-scale liquidity measures to ensure a sustained supply of credit to the real economy and to support financial intermediation. While financial conditions have eased in domestic and foreign currency markets, the global financial system remains vulnerable to another round of liquidity strains triggered by adverse scenarios (Financial Stability Board 2020).

Credit losses and liquidity constraints are exacerbated by operational issues arising from increased reliance on digital technology, not only for providing banking services, but also transitioning to remote working models. Social distancing measures led to branch closures, which stressed digital channels and systems and overwhelmed contact centers working on a work-from-home basis. While banks that invested in technologies, such as cloud, open application programming interface architecture, artificial intelligence, security, and mobility managed to weather the impact of social distancing measures, banks that have not had a forward-looking approach to digital transformation are at a disadvantage. Late adopters of digital transformation are at risk of losing market share or at worst at risk of closure (Silva 2020).

While the banking sector is in a stronger position due to macroprudential policies implemented in the aftermath of the global financial crisis, international institutions still expect a sharp rise in NPLs in the near term amid adverse scenarios and cessation of forbearance measures. Table 3 shows that NPL ratios in most economies in the Asian region are below 10%. However, NPL ratios rose during the third quarter of 2020. While initial NPLs rose slightly in the first quarter of 2020 (Table 4), the true extent of the NPL issue might not be captured in the immediate term as economies aim to enhance liquidity and mitigate the impacts on the real sector through temporary regulatory forbearance (e.g., debt moratorium) and accommodative monetary policy stances. For example, Asian economies such as Malaysia and Thailand extended a 6-month debt moratorium on SME loans to retain employment and maintain business stability.[6]

Table 3: Nonperforming Loan Ratios, Selected Asian Economies
(%)

Economy	Sep 2019	Dec 2019	Mar 2020	Jun 2020	Sep 2020
Central Asia					
Armenia	5.45	5.51	5.52	5.68	6.01
Kazakhstan	9.34	8.13	9.41	8.97	8.35
Kyrgyz Republic	8.35	8.00	8.35	8.60	9.66
Tajikistan	31.50	27.00	29.20	31.00	28.50
East Asia					
China, People's Republic of	1.86	1.86	1.91	1.94	1.96
Hong Kong, China	0.60	0.60	0.60	0.79	0.84
Korea, Republic of	0.41	0.38	0.39	0.37	0.35
Mongolia	10.87	10.09	10.69	11.04	11.36
South Asia					
Bangladesh	11.99	9.30	9.00	9.16	8.88
India	9.10	9.20	8.43	8.16	7.70
Maldives	9.60	9.40	9.10	9.30	9.00
Pakistan	1.38	1.34	1.51	1.45	1.26
Sri Lanka	4.90	4.70	5.10	5.30	5.43
Southeast Asia					
Brunei Darussalam	5.00	4.79	4.51	4.44	4.48
Cambodia	1.87	1.55	1.77	2.17	2.31
Indonesia	2.66	2.53	2.77	3.11	3.14
Malaysia	1.61	1.52	1.59	1.46	1.38
Philippines	2.15	2.04	2.25	2.57	3.51
Thailand	3.16	3.13	3.21	3.22	3.27
Viet Nam	1.94	1.63	1.77	1.80	2.14

Note: White cells denote nonperforming ratio less than 5%, yellow between 5% and 10%, and orange higher than 10%.

Source: CEIC Database https://www.ceicdata.com/en (accessed on 2 February 2021).

---

[6] See the ADB COVID-19 Policy Database for a complete list of forbearance measures in Asia, at https://covid19policy.adb.org/policy-measures

Table 4: Percent Changes of Nonperforming Loans (2019 Q4–2020 Q2), Selected Asian Economies
(%)

	PRC	Thailand	Philippines	Indonesia	Malaysia	Brunei Darussalam
Q2 2020 (A)	386,407.3	16,334.1	5,461.4	12.2	6,153.0	181.9
Q1 2020 (B)	368,855.8	15,942.0	4,974.0	11.2	6,617.4	188.7
Q4 2019 (C)	340,812.8	14,922.6	4,473.4	10.0	6,344.1	196.2
Percent changes =((A–C)/C)*100	13.4%	9.5%	22.1%	21.7%	–3.0%	–7.3%

PRC = People's Republic of China, Q = quarter.

Note: Figures are in United States dollar currency in millions and data is restricted to six economies that had reported June 2020 nonperforming loan figures as of 8 September 2020.

Source: CEIC data. https://www.ceicdata.com/en (accessed 4 September 2020).

Alongside regulatory forbearance, central banks have continuously eased monetary policy, lowering policy rates and putting downward pressure on long-term interest rates and promoting greater lending to businesses and households (Figure 4). With the expected increase in NPLs already putting pressure on bank profitability, low rates will continue to reduce net interest margins and overall bank profitability. The International Monetary Fund (IMF) forecasts that a persistent period of low interest rates is likely to further pressure bank profitability, with a large fraction of banks failing to generate profits above their cost of equity until 2025 (IMF 2020). Together, rising NPLs and low interest rates will impair banks' general capital and capital adequacy ratio thresholds, which will severely constrain capacity to provide loans to the real sector and activate corrective action and even resolution mechanisms (Carletti et al. 2020, Awad et al. 2020).

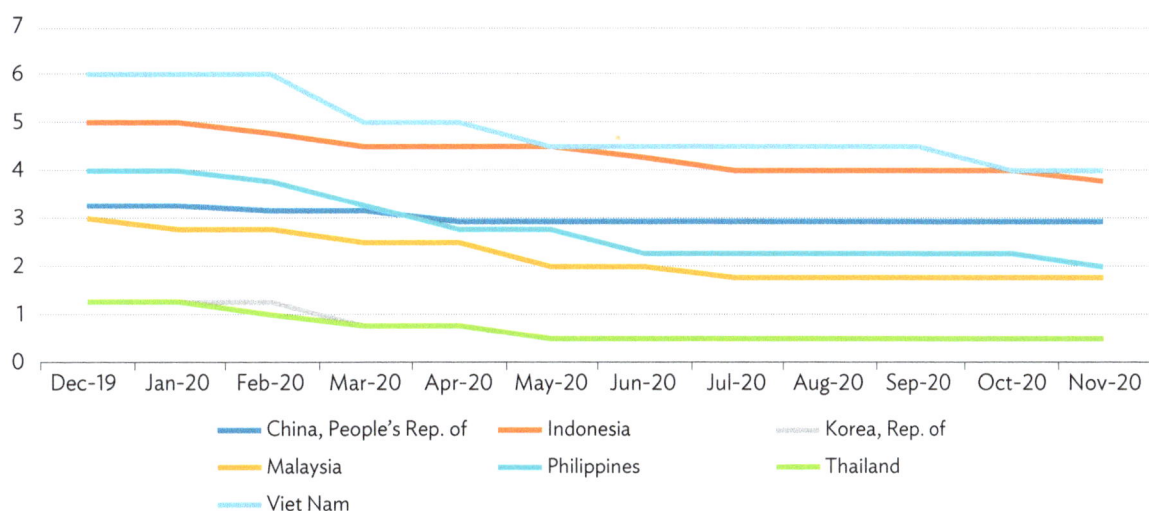

Figure 4: Policy Rate Changes in Selected Asian Economies
(%)

Source: Asian Development Bank. 2020. *Asian Bond Monitor – November 2020*. Manila.

Capital Markets

The economic effects of decreasing market confidence, in addition to social-distancing measures to contain the virus, have slashed global economic growth forecasts and led to financial market turmoil that far outweighs the effects of the global financial crisis. Stock markets in major economies declined over 30% in March 2020, implied volatilities of equities spiked to crisis levels, and credit spreads on non-investment grade debt widened sharply as investors reduced risks (Figure 5) (OECD 2020). The Chicago Board Options Exchange Volatility Index (VIX)[7] jumped to crisis levels similar to the global financial crisis, with a peak of 82.69 on 16 March 2020.[8] Though VIX levels have been decreasing since then, fears of a resurgence in COVID-19 cases and an expected slow recovery have left volatility expectations elevated, as seen by the resurgence starting on 11 June 2020.

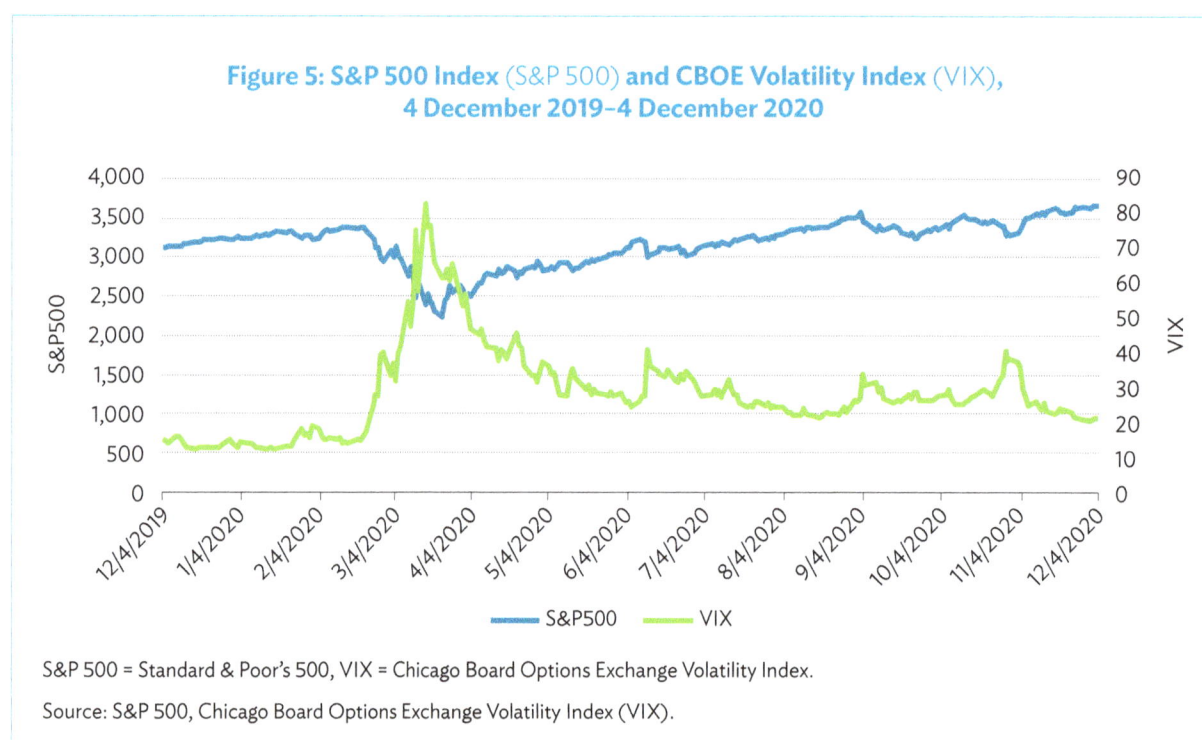

Figure 5: S&P 500 Index (S&P 500) and CBOE Volatility Index (VIX), 4 December 2019–4 December 2020

S&P 500 = Standard & Poor's 500, VIX = Chicago Board Options Exchange Volatility Index.

Source: S&P 500, Chicago Board Options Exchange Volatility Index (VIX).

In March 2020 as the impact of COVID-19 began in earnest, assets sold off sharply amid heightened risk aversion and tight global financial conditions (Figure 6). Data from the Institute of International Finance indicate that nonresident equity flows to emerging Asia dropped $13 billion in March 2020 and another $17 billion in April 2020. Emerging market economies, including in East Asia,[9] felt the brunt of these selloffs as international investors sought safe-haven assets, such as US Treasuries, spurred on by tightening global financial conditions starting already in February 2020. Investors typically prefer such assets during crisis as they are liquid and protect them from stock market losses (Cheema and Szulczyk 2020).

---

[7] The Chicago Board Options Exchange Volatility Index, or VIX, is a real-time market index of market expectations of 30-day forward-looking volatility.

[8] VIX peaked at 80.86 in 2008 during the global financial crisis.

[9] Emerging market economies in Asia include the PRC, India, Indonesia, Malaysia, the Philippines, Sri Lanka, and Thailand (IMF 2021).

Figure 6: Total Portfolio Flows in Selected Asian Economies
(raw data in $ million; proxy for balance of payments portfolio flows)

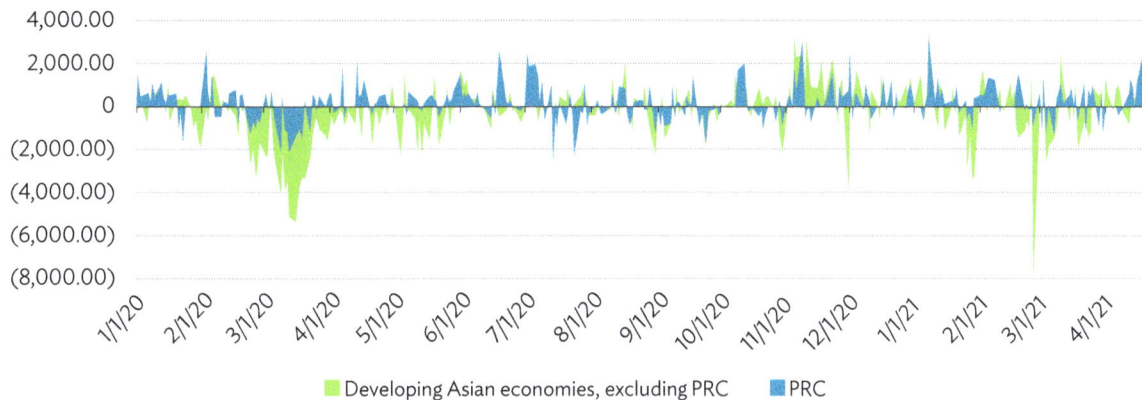

Developing Asian economies, excluding PRC   PRC

PRC = People's Republic of China.

Note: Asian developing economies included in the figure are restricted to emerging markets included in the Institute of International Finance's database. These include the People's Republic of China; Indonesia; India; the Republic of Korea; Malaysia; Pakistan; the Philippines; Sri Lanka; Taipei,China; Thailand; Viet Nam.

Source: Institute of International Finance. IIF Daily Flows Database. https://www.iif.com/Research/Capital-Flows-and-Debt (accessed 19 April 2021).

Due to higher demand for safe-haven assets such as US Treasuries, most East Asian currencies depreciated against the US dollar, and financial conditions deteriorated as equity markets declined, credit spreads widened, and capital flowed out of local currency bonds (ADB 2020c). Indeed, throughout the pandemic so far, emerging Asian currencies lost value against the US dollar (except for outliers such as the Philippines and Thailand) (Table 5). Such action erodes the capital gains of foreign investors and may trigger further capital outflows and worsen domestic financial conditions as emerging market local currency bond spreads rise (Park, Rosenkranz, and Tayag 2020). Additionally, the lack of foreign exchange risk hedge mechanisms in Asia reduces investor appetite and market volatility (Kang and Tian 2020). This is a concern in most emerging Asian economies, as the narrow and weak institutional investor base leads to heavy reliance on foreign investment and higher exposure to financial strains. Park, Rosenkranz, and Tayag (2020) estimate that a widening in the cross-currency basis swap is significantly and positively related to nonresident capital outflows driven by debt and bank flows.

At the onset of the crisis, local currency bond markets experienced outsized portfolio outflows amid risk aversion and profit taking as yields in those markets declined as central banks cut rates (ADB 2020c). Emerging Asia experienced a large-scale decline in foreign investor holdings and an increase in registered net outflows that persisted in some countries until the third quarter of 2020 (Table 6). Nevertheless, emerging East Asia's local currency bond market expanded to $18.7 trillion at the end of September 2020 on growth of 4.8% quarter-on-quarter and 17.4% year-on-year in the third quarter of 2020 driven by increasing financing need from the public and private sectors. As of the end of September 2020, government bonds comprised 61.6% of the region's total local currency bonds—amounting to $11.5 trillion. Local currency bond market growth was hampered by the deceleration in corporate bond market due to rising interest rates. The whole region experienced –0.6% quarter-on-quarter growth but corporate debt was up 24.3% year-on-year in (Table 7) (ADB 2020d).

Table 5: Changes in Financial Conditions
(2020)

Country	February–May		August–November	
	FX (%)	Equity Market (%)	FX (%)	Equity Market (%)
China, People's Republic of	–2.0	–1.0	3.6	–2.5
Indonesia	–2.0	–12.8	2.5	1.9
Malaysia	–3.0	–0.6	0.8	–0.4
Philippines	0.7	–14.0	0.3	13.6
Singapore	–1.4	–16.6	0.9	1.8
Korea, Republic of	–1.8	2.1	6.0	3.9
Thailand	–0.9	0.2	1.5	–3.9
Viet Nam	–0.2	–2.0	–0.004	6.4

FX = foreign exchange.

Note: A negative (positive) value in foreign exchange indicates appreciation (depreciation) against the United States dollar.

Source: ADB. 2020. Asian Bond Monitor – June 2020, Asian Bond Monitor – November 2020. Manila.

Table 6: Changes in Foreign Holdings in Local Currency Bond Markets
(% of total)

Country	Q4 2019	Q1 2020	Q2 2020	Q3 2020	Q4 2020
China, People's Republic of	8.54	8.68	9.09	9.36	–
Indonesia	38.57	32.71	30.17	26.96	25.16
Japan	12.89	12.86	12.83	12.63	–
Korea, Republic of	12.47	12.79	13.05	13.34	–
Malaysia	25.29	44.3	22.73	23.55	–
Philippines	4.88	3.91	1.91	1.54	–
Thailand	16.97	15.30	14.43	13.99	–
Viet Nam	0.78	0.72	0.59	0.55	–

– = data not available during time of access, Q = quarter.

Source: *AsianBondsOnline*. https://asianbondsonline.adb.org/ (accessed 2 February 2021).

Table 7: Local Currency Corporate Debt Market

Economy	Q2 2020 ($ billion)	Q3 2020 ($ billion)	Growth Rate (quarter-on-quarter, %)
China, People's Republic of	678	707	0.2
Hong Kong, China	30	28	−8.2
Indonesia	1	3	340.7
Korea, Republic of	112	104	−8.9
Malaysia	8	9	12.1
Philippines	1	3	358.3
Singapore	4	4	−16.1
Thailand	8	10	27.4
Viet Nam	4	3	−19.3

Q = quarter.

Source: ADB (2020). *Asian Bond Monitor – November 2020*. Manila.

Bond yields across Asia declined (Table 8) amid (i) accommodative central bank policies such as interest rate cuts and other quantitative easing policies, and (ii) lower risk perception for government assets compared to corporate bonds that are exposed to COVID-19's effects (ADB 2020c). The performance of 10-year bond yields across the region has remained mixed, however. Investor concern about government announcements and downgrades on the sovereign rating outlook contributed to a rise in 10-year bond yields (ADB 2020c).

Table 8: Two-Year and Ten-Year Government Bond Yields

Economy	2-Year Government Bond (bps)	10-Year Government Bond (bps)
China, People's Rep. of	38	18
Hong Kong, China	−13	−4
Indonesia	−20	−57
Japan	−3	−3
Korea, Republic of	−2	4
Malaysia	−0.7	−8
Philippines	−6	19
Singapore	2	−23
Thailand	3	−11
Viet Nam	−9	−32

bps = basis points.

Source: ADB (2020). *Asian Bond Monitor – November 2020*. Manila.

Equity markets in emerging Asia posted large losses at the onset of the pandemic as investors grew more risk averse (Table 5). In May 2020, however, markets in economies such as Indonesia (1.9%), the Philippines (13.6%), Singapore (1.8%), and Viet Nam (6.4%) gained slightly or stabilized as of November 2020 due to effective containment measures or lifting of lockdown measures. Countries such as the PRC (−2.5%), Malaysia (−0.4%), and Thailand (−3.9%), in contrast, still posted large losses from August to November 2020.

However, capital market conditions have been very different since March 2020. For instance, fears about the economic turmoil caused by the COVID-19 pandemic caused high-yield, municipal, and corporate investment-grade bond yields to rise significantly. In March 2020, spreads on high-yield bonds topped more than 1,000 basis points. Since April 2020, spreads have fallen steadily and are almost at pre-pandemic levels (Figure 7). In November 2020, high-yield bonds yielded less than 500 basis points, below where they were at the end of 2019. Also, improved investment sentiment has led to a decline in credit default swap spreads in most emerging East Asian markets since March 2020 (Table 9) (ADB 2020c). Credit default swap values declined about −52.6% on average during the period of 30 March 2020 to 31 December 2020.

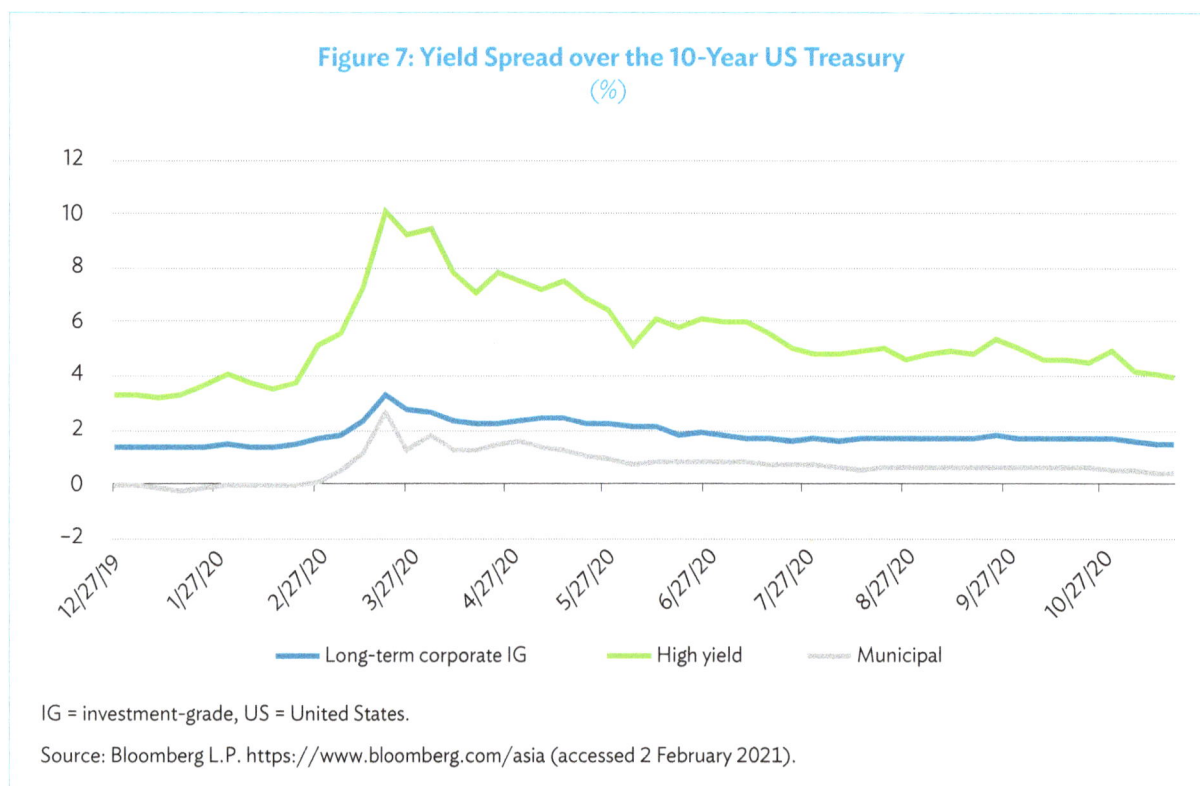

Figure 7: Yield Spread over the 10-Year US Treasury
(%)

IG = investment-grade, US = United States.

Source: Bloomberg L.P. https://www.bloomberg.com/asia (accessed 2 February 2021).

Table 9: Five-Year Credit Default Swap Value for Select Countries, 30 March 2020–31 December 2020

Country	Q1 2020	Q4 2020	Growth rate (%)
China, People's Rep. of	61.82	27.97	–54.74
Japan	41.94	15.10	–64.00
Korea, Republic of	42.75	21.97	–48.60
Indonesia	239.11	67.51	–71.80
India*	221.68	107.14	–51.70
Malaysia*	120.09	57.19	–52.40
Pakistan*	691.00	505.92	–26.80
Philippines*	109.88	57.35	–47.80
Germany	22.94	10.70	–53.40
United States	16.58	12.70	–23.40

Q = quarter.

* 29 September 2020 is the last data available.

Source: World Government Bonds, http://www.worldgovernmentbonds.com/

As of end 2020, stock markets in major economies around the world were also in very different situations than they were as COVID-19 broke in March 2020. Shares in India; Japan; Indonesia; Hong Kong, China; Europe; the PRC; and the US had climbed about 35.4% on average (Table 10). Markets expect this situation to continue for a considerable time. This is because the US Federal Open Market Committee in January 2021 reaffirmed its commitment to using its full range of powers to support the economic recovery at its current pace. The Fed Funds rate will remain anchored in a range between 0% and 0.25% (CNBC News 2021).

Table 10: Stock Index Increases in Major Economies, 30 March–31 December 2020

Economy	Index	Q1 2020	Q4 2020	Growth Rate (%)
China, People's Rep. of	SSE	2,750.30	3,473.07	26.3
India	BSE 30	29,468.49	47,746.22	62.0
Japan	Nikkei 225	18,917.01	27,444.17	45.1
Korea, Republic of	KOSPI	1,997	2,613	30.8
Indonesia	IDX	4,538.93	5,979.07	31.7
Hong Kong, China	Hang Seng	23,603.48	27,231.13	15.4
Europe	Euro Stoxx 50	2,786.90	3,552.64	27.5
United States	Dow Jones Industrial	21,917.16	30,606.48	39.6

IDX = Indonesian Stock Exchange Index, KOSPI = Korean Stock Exchange Index, Q = quarter, SSE = Shanghai Stock Exchange.

Source: Authors' compilation.

Due to governments' ongoing liquidity support and the maintenance of ultra-low interest rates, many stock markets are experiencing an unprecedented boom (Avalos and Xia 2020). However, concerns are mounting that capital markets are not reflecting sluggish real economies. To stem the impact of COVID-19, unprecedented monetary policy actions have driven asset prices up by causing a sharp drop in both risk premiums and risk-free discount rates. It is true that governments cannot continue current support measures. Experience from previous crisis suggest that a premature withdrawal of policy stimulus could hinder a sustained economic recovery. Policy measures should not be withdrawn until there is clear evidence of financial stability and resurgence in private demand (IMF 2010).

Insurance and Pensions

COVID-19 has hurt the insurance and pensions sector in Asia. The response to the pandemic holds key financial implications for insurers, including uncertainty in revenues due to lower or delayed renewals and a decline in new business, increased claim frequency and severity, capital impacts, as well as changing risk profiles and business mixes. In some cases, premium refunds on cancelled policies, such as travel insurance, compounds the problem.

Market valuations have suffered in line with the broader financial markets, but technical performance is unlikely to deteriorate materially. The most significant prudential impact on the insurance sector has been on solvency and profitability, primarily through losses on the asset side. Due to riskier asset allocation, insurers are likely to experience falling bond yields and more declines in return on equity than developed markets, due to volatility in capital markets. In addition, low interest rates pose a risk to insurers' investment performance, especially life insurers with guaranteed back books. The low interest rate environment is also likely to have negative impact on the investment yields of non-life insurers to a lesser extent. Both these factors weigh on insurers' profitability, both return on assets and equity. Prolonged stress on equity and credit markets, combined with declines in interest rates, are likely to weaken earnings and erode the capital headroom of reinsurers. Nevertheless, solvency ratios have generally remained well above jurisdictional requirements. In terms of liquidity, the data suggest that the impact has been limited, raising no immediate concern for the sector's ability to fulfill obligations at this point. However, vulnerabilities remain, given uncertainties about the duration and impact of the COVID-19 crisis. These vulnerabilities include the potential for decreasing credit quality of insurers' fixed-income portfolios and the impact of the further deterioration in the low-yield environment.

The impact of the pandemic in the sector has varied based on the line of business; indeed, on the liability side, it varies greatly based on this factor. It has impacted insurers with more diversified portfolios less.

Life insurance

(i) A spike in COVID-related life insurance (mortality) claims has impacted most life insurers across the region. In addition, Figure 8 shows the results of a poll conducted by GlobalData last December 2020. Around 19% of the respondents believe that life and health products would increase due to COVID-19 as individuals and businesses feel vulnerable to the virus and want more protection in the form of such policies. Thus, GlobalData projects that the life insurance written premium in the Asia and Pacific region will reach $1.5 trillion in 2023 as life insurers offer COVID-19 specific riders and extended additional relief measures for policyholders diagnosed with the COVID-19 (Figure 9). Therefore, the insurance sector will be facing more pandemic-related claims as the demand for life insurance policies increase.

(ii) Rising unemployment may increase claims from income protection insurance, subject to policy limitations.

(iii) Some finance sector assessment programs include a pandemic scenario as part of stress tests on life insurers, which showed little impact on the insurance liabilities of the insurance sector. However, life insurers with more longevity risk (e.g., guaranteed annuities) will experience a reduction in risk profile, as mortality rates increase.

Figure 8: COVID-19's Impact to the Insurance Sector
(%)

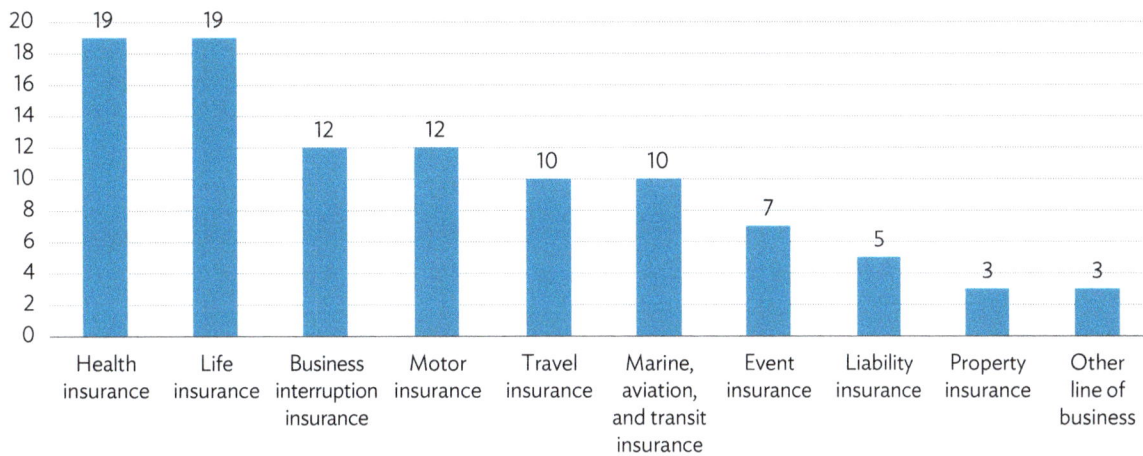

COVID-19 = coronavirus disease.

Source: GlobalData Insurance Intelligence Center. https://www.globaldata.com/ (accessed 23 June 2021).

Figure 9: Asia and Pacific Life Insurance Market

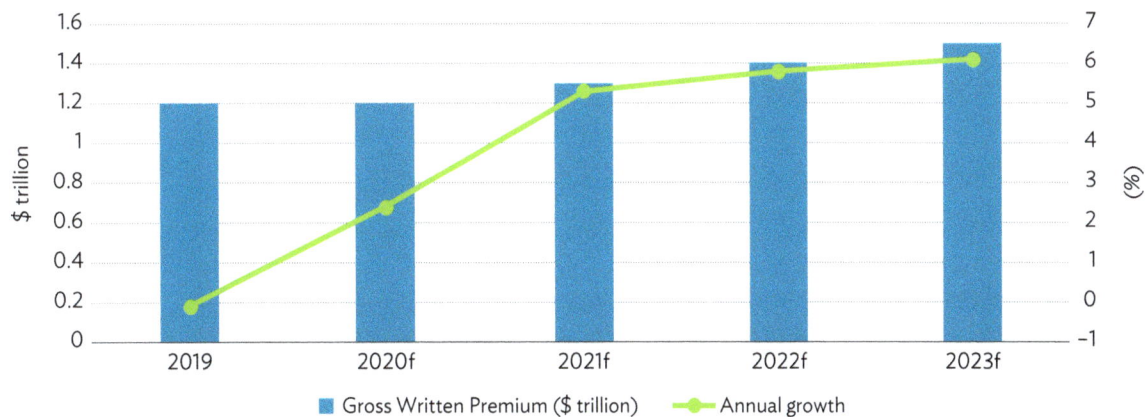

Gross Written Premium ($ trillion)   Annual growth

f = forecast.

Source: GlobalData Insurance Intelligence Center, https://www.globaldata.com/ (accessed 23 June 2021).

Health insurance

(i) Although the penetration of private health insurance is relatively low, a volume-driven spike in medical claims could be a significant cost for private insurers in many developing Asian economies with large vulnerable populations, such as India and Indonesia. Furthermore, the COVID-19 pandemic underlined the need for health insurance in emerging markets as public health care institutions struggled with surge in demand, forcing individuals to seek faster treatment through private insurance instead. Hence, GlobalData's insight report reveals that personal accident and health insurance written premium in Asia and the Pacific is forecasted to grow up to $240.1 billion in 2023 as COVID-19 accelerated the demand for private insurers (Figure 10). Due to this, the health maintenance organization industry under the insurance sector may deal with a tremendous amount of COVID-related claims in the future. In countries where most medical expenses from COVID-19-related treatment are currently being borne by governments, e.g., Japan, the Republic of Korea, the PRC, and Singapore, the relative impact will be limited.

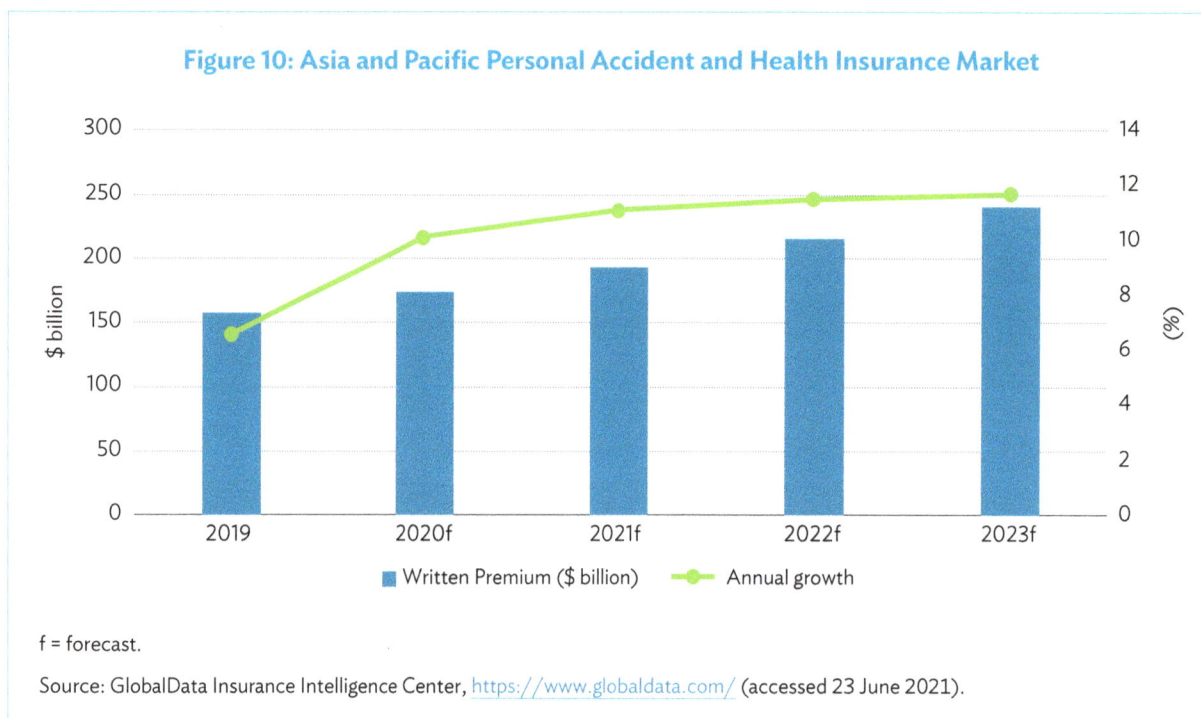

Figure 10: Asia and Pacific Personal Accident and Health Insurance Market

f = forecast.

Source: GlobalData Insurance Intelligence Center, https://www.globaldata.com/ (accessed 23 June 2021).

Non-life insurance

(i) Liability lines: Trade, credit, bond, and surety insurance has been hit hard, due to delayed trade settlements, the drying-up of credit facilities, and insolvencies. This is despite widespread interventions by most governments, banks, and credit institutions to limit or delay the stress to financial systems. Given the increasing risks brought by the COVID-19 pandemic, GlobalData has estimated the liability insurance industry to grow up to $33.4 billion in 2023, in terms of written premiums, as the demand for liability insurance rise (Figure 11).

Figure 11: Asia and Pacific Liability Insurance Market

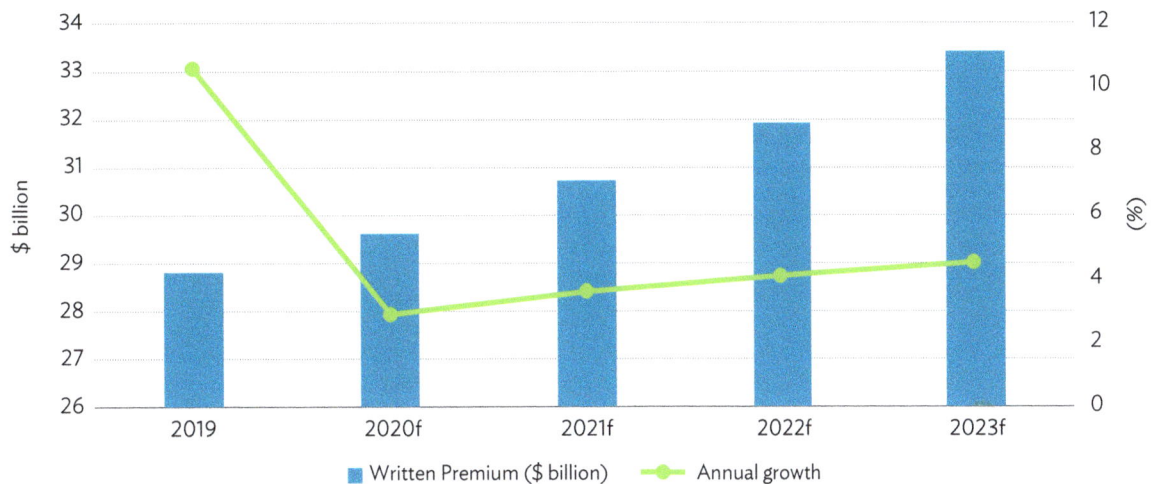

f = forecast.

Source: GlobalData Insurance Intelligence Center, https://www.globaldata.com/ (accessed 23 June 2021).

(ii) Business interruption: Even though the pandemic has directly impacted a lot of businesses, claims are expected to be limited. This is because these insurance policies normally cover property losses but not disease outbreaks. Moreover, they often exclude "extraordinary events," "forced business closures imposed by authorities," and "infectious diseases." Employees infected by a virus while at work are likely to file workers' injury claims to cover loss of income or medical expenses under workmen's compensation insurance. Organizations providing essential services—such as medical facilities, airports, and utilities—are particularly vulnerable to such claims. Although most governments in Asia are funding COVID-related treatment costs, claims costs are increasingly likely to surge in the future.

(iii) Event cancellation: The cancellation or postponement of numerous events, such the Tokyo Olympics, are likely to trigger event cancellation claims. Not all events, especially the smaller ones, are insured, and some policies carry pandemic exclusions. In spite of relatively few claims, the total amount could still be quite significant: for example, the Tokyo Olympics has cumulative insurance cover of more than $2 billion in total.

(iv) Personal lines. Claims related to personal insurance have been significantly lower due to lockdown restrictions, e.g., widespread drops in car usage have translated into fewer accidents and confining people to their homes has reduced property theft.

Pensions

(i)   Pension schemes have been impacted through a number of channels. The main ones are: (i) increased likelihood of individuals exiting the labor market and claiming pension benefits; (ii) labor market effects resulting in declining wages; (iii) asset price shocks hurting funded pension schemes' balance sheets; and (iv) capacity of governments and private enterprises, as underwriters of pension obligations, to maintain the solvency of defined benefit pension schemes. The severity of the financial and welfare consequences suffered by scheme underwriters and members depends on the scheme's precrisis financial position. Since, on average, 70% of employment is informal, in Asia, one would expect the long-term impact of these developments on baseline pension expenditures to be low. However, the initial expenditure shock may remain for years and contribute to further increases in the short-term fiscal pressures arising from the crisis.

(ii) The potential impact on Pacific pension and provident funds is much more foreboding, as these institutions fill the gaps left by an underdeveloped domestic credit market. Even before the pandemic, Pacific pension funds acknowledged the need for withdrawals and are utilized as emergency saving funds against life's contingencies, such as natural hazards. However, the impact of the pandemic on employment and insolvency poses a larger risk, as withdrawals exacerbate liquidity issues posed by unemployment, lower investment returns due to lower interest rates and reduced dividends, and depressed asset prices (Pacific Sector Development Initiative 2020). Specifically, withdrawals during the pandemic have been more severe as funds may be forced to realize value losses if they liquidate assets in a bear market (Feher and Bidegain 2020). While withdrawal policies are helpful during the pandemic, these undermine the long-term adequacy of pension benefits and policy makers should ensure the sustainability and replenishment of these funds after the recovery period (Juergens and Galvani 2020).

Exposure to disaster events due to natural hazards, as well as other perils, and the potential for an increase in frequency of catastrophe events, can also lead to earnings volatility. Asia and the Pacific is host to commercial, manufacturing, and logistics hubs dotted with small business enterprises. They are all highly exposed to disasters caused by natural hazards. Low investments in disaster resilience and business continuity management expose them to physical damage and economic losses to production facilities. The substantial impacts of the COVID-19 pandemic have added to the expanding disaster risks in the region. As the pandemic spread during the first half of the year, the virus interacted with natural hazards in the cyclone and monsoon season, creating significant challenges for critical infrastructure such as hospitals, safe shelter and housing, utilities, water and sanitation, and transport. In addition, the financial consequences of natural hazards include the destruction of property and equipment, damage to stock, revenue loss, and rising operational costs.

3 Immediate Policy Responses to the Impacts of the Pandemic Crisis

Governments have been quick to respond to the crisis, implementing unprecedented fiscal, monetary, and emergency liquidity actions to mitigate the painful economic and financial shocks of the pandemic. In the real sector, policy makers have implemented a slew of social protection policies to protect vulnerable households. They also implemented targeted liquidity and tax relief measures for MSMEs/SMEs. In the finance sector, governments quickly realized the crucial role of financial intermediation in risk mitigation and post-pandemic recovery. They thus have implemented immediate and short-term accommodative monetary and financial policies and measures to ease financial stress and liquidity concerns rapidly in the banking and nonbank finance sector such as policy rate cuts and forbearance measures.

Social Protection and Jobs Programs

Income security is necessary to lead a dignified life, especially for poor and vulnerable households. Given the significant health and economic hardships to households during the pandemic, adequate and immediate assistance is crucial to such households and must be sustained for as long as necessary and possible.

Social protection schemes have been important in the coordinated policy response to COVID-19. Coordinated social protection, active labor market policies, and job creation programs are essential to strong, speedy, and sustainable recovery (ILO 2020b). By generating greater consumption across economies, it can reduce the depth recession and the risks of escalating social tensions, enabling countries to recover more quickly (Kidd, Athias, and Tran 2020).

As of 16 November 2020, 209 countries (94% of 222 countries in the world) had introduced or adapted 1,568 social protection and jobs programs in response to the pandemic (ILO 2020c). The majority of these programs (54%) are new and attempt to bridge large social protection gaps in low to middle-income countries (ILO 2020c). The most common measures so far include special social allowance/grants (16.6%), followed by programs on income and jobs protection (14.7%) (Table 11) (ILO 2020c). Unemployment protection schemes, in conjunction with cash disbursements to low- and middle-income groups, can ensure continued household consumption, ensure the credit quality of retail borrowers, and act as social, economic, and financial stabilizers.

Table 11: Measures Announced, by Social Protection Function
(%)

Special allowance/grant	16.6
Income/jobs protection	14.7
Several functions	11.8
Health	10.8
Unemployment protection	10.7
Housing/basic services	8.8
Food and nutrition	8.2
Children and family	7.8
Pensions	5.5
Sickness	3.7
Access to education	0.7
Maternity/parental	0.4
Employment injury	0.2

Source: ILO. COVID-19 Social Protection Monitor, https://www.social-protection.org (accessed November 2020).

However, while the rest of the world has taken the right step in creating or expanding social protection schemes to combat the pandemic, Asia and the Pacific lags, with 13% of countries in the region making no social protection response (ILO 2020c). Underdeveloped and weak social security systems have limited the capacity of Asian economies to adequately respond to the COVID-19 crisis. In many countries, the pre-COVID-19 paradigm of supporting those traditionally regarded as poor and vulnerable has limited the scope of policy responses, often excluding about half of the most vulnerable groups (Kidd, Athias, and Tran 2020). For example, most informal workers are unregistered, making it difficult for authorities to reach disadvantaged groups in the informal economy (ILO 2020d). The "missing middle"—which includes households not considered "poor enough," such as formal economy workers that lost their jobs and have recently become poor and vulnerable—fails to qualify for social assistance benefits (Kidd, Athias, and Tran 2020).

Remittances

Declining remittance inflows has also raised significant risks for migrants and their families, especially for Asia's developing countries where the remittances-to-GDP ratio is relatively high. Countries have adopted a significant number of proactive measures to solve declining remittance inflows, along with global collaborative efforts.

Many developing countries have ensured that money transfer operators have remained open and accessible under lockdown by designating them essential services so funds can be sent and received by benefactors. Costs levied by service providers were reduced. Pakistan made particular effort to ensure remittances continued flowing by changing the threshold for fee-free transactions from $200 to $100. In Bangladesh, a bonus payment of 2% of the transfer value was introduced for receipt of formal remittances. In Sri Lanka, authorities implemented regulatory easing and tax exemptions for inward remittances and Nepal Rastra Bank has been encouraging digital remittance transfers to bank accounts, in addition to raising the limit placed on fund transfer amounts (knomad n.d.).[10] Source countries have contributed to these efforts by providing medical assistance and employment assistance through retention and hiring of laid-off migrant workers. In Thailand, migrant workers with expired contracts were allowed to stay in the country without the need for extension of permits (Takenaka et al. 2020).

Along with such efforts at the individual country level, global collaboration is underway. In 2020, the United Kingdom and Swiss authorities called for countries around the world to support fund inflows to developing countries during the COVID-19 pandemic through easing of regulations concerning international money transfer access and support for scaling of digital channels. A number of countries including Australia, Cambodia, Pakistan, and Vanuatu as well as organizations such as ADB, the World Bank, UN Capital Development Fund, United Nations Development Programme and the International Organization for Migration have supported this call to action (Donkin 2020).

While not exhaustive, Table 12 lists policy actions worth considering in uplifting the welfare of migrants and ensuring the continuous flow of remittances.

Table 12: Potential Policy Actions

Improve safety and welfare of migrant workers and their families	• Provide migrant workers access to compensatory benefits or other emergency relief programs targeted at COVID-19-affected workers in host countries. • Assist stranded, laid-off, or other distressed migrant workers and provide necessary humanitarian, health, legal, and administrative support. • Use diplomatic missions to ensure welfare, wages, and benefits for migrant workers staying in host countries.
Facilitate employment retention and placement	• Facilitate convenient and safe processes in renewal of work permits. • Incentivize employers to retain migrant workforce. • Facilitate employment placement of laid-off migrant workers.
Facilitate reintegration of returned migrants	• Provide an emergency cash transfer. • Ensure employment opportunity and foster entrepreneurship among repatriated migrant workers. • Initiate online job matching of unemployed overseas workers and conduct training programs to enhance their employability.
Ensure flow of remittances	• Recognize remittance service providers as an essential service exempted for restrictions. • Create supportive business environment through relaxing regulations (e.g., tax breaks, compliance) and reducing remittance fees. • Facilitate use of digital platforms in sending and receiving remittances. • Address knowledge and data gap.
Promote and incentivize digital remittances	• Develop a structured and consistent approach to implement digital remittance solutions taking into account the need for infrastructure, identification, anti-money laundering/combating the financing of terrorism and regulations. • Increase financial education of digital services. • Regulators, financial institutions, and money transfer operators should work together to safeguard remittances and promote competition and innovation. • Enabling interoperable systems leading to fair access to market players and more affordable and efficient transactions.

Sources: Asian Development Bank compilation; Asian Development Bank. 2020. COVID-19 Impact on International Migration, Remittances, and Recipient Households in Developing Asia. *ADB Brief*. 148. Manila.

---

[10] Impact of COVID-19 on remittances (knomad.org).

Another challenge with remittances is de-risking, which also limits correspondent banking relationships and trade flows. The pandemic has amplified de-risking, a problem in Asia and the Pacific since 2012, which refers to when financial institutions terminate or restrict business relationships with clients to avoid risk, rather than manage it. This reverses progress in reducing costs, strengthening safety, and enhancing security of remittance flows. Further, it moves high-risk transactions from the regulated system into informal channels (Isaacs 2021).

To tackle the negative side effects of de-risking, some central banks and multilateral organizations have collaborated to develop a know-your-customer (KYC) tool and approach. The World Bank financed a national digital identification system, for example, to provide digital ID to first-generation Samoan migrants in Australia and New Zealand, the key sources of remittances to Samoa. The national digital identification will ensure KYC compliance for the remittance channels (World Bank n.d.). In addition, the South Pacific Central Bank Governors approved a regional KYC utility to enable low-cost identification of senders and recipients of financial transactions in the Pacific. The utility will comply with international standards to counter money laundering and financing of terrorism. Moreover, through the establishment of a regional KYC project, remittance payments will be properly facilitated while correspondent banking relationships for small banks and money transfer operators will be preserved. This utility is overseen by a steering committee made up of representatives of the nine South Pacific central banks, and co-chaired by authorities from the Reserve Bank of Australia and the Reserve Bank of New Zealand, with the IMF and Pacific Financial Technical Assistance Centre (Pacific Financial Technical Assistance Centre 2020).

Micro, Small, and Medium-Sized Enterprises

SMEs form the backbone of developing economies. Supporting MSMEs is thus vital in preserving employment and for the quick recovery of economies and has been a key focus of urgent government stimulus packages globally. World Bank's MSME support tracker reports 1,600 policies supporting MSMEs globally. The most widely used instruments in response to the outbreak are debt finance (594), employment support (358), and tax subsidies (314).[11] Similarly, across Asia and the Pacific, the most used policies are debt finance (205), tax relief (119), and employment support (73) (Table 13).

---

[11] World Bank. Map of SME-Support Measures in Response to COVID-19. https://www.worldbank.org/en/data/interactive/2020/04/14/map-of-sme-support-measures-in-response-to-covid-19 (accessed 9 March 2021).

**Table 13: Small and Medium-Sized Enterprise Policies in Developing Economies
in Asia and the Pacific**

Region	CWRD	EARD	PARD	SARD	SERD	TOTAL
Tax	4	34	8	13	60	119
Business costs	1	16	1	6	45	69
Business advice	1	9	0	1	3	14
Debt finance	8	44	5	22	126	205
Other finance	3	3	1	0	9	16
Employment support	8	17	4	5	39	73
Demand	0	8	1	2	15	26
Business climate	0	9	1	2	15	27
TOTAL	**25**	**140**	**21**	**51**	**312**	**549**

Notes: Economies included in the database for each region include: Central and West Asia = Armenia, Georgia, Kazakhstan, Pakistan, Uzbekistan; East Asia = the People's Republic of China; Hong Kong, China; the Republic of Korea; Mongolia; Pacific = Fiji, Papua New Guinea, Vanuatu; South Asia = Bangladesh, India, Nepal, Sri Lanka; Southeast Asia = Brunei Darussalam, Cambodia, Indonesia, the Lao People's Democratic Republic, Malaysia, the Philippines, Singapore, Thailand, Viet Nam.

Source: World Bank. Map of MSME-Support Measures in Response to COVID-19. https://www.worldbank.org/en/data/interactive/2020/04/14/map-of-sme-support-measures-in-response-to-covid-19 (accessed 9 March 2021).

Under debt finance measures, the most commonly implemented instruments are new lending (78) and delayed repayments (42) (Table 14). Most Asian governments have implemented debt moratorium measures to bridge the financial difficulties that illiquid but viable businesses are experiencing during the containment of the pandemic. Asian governments have issued guidelines on loan payment deferment for SMEs and relaxed regulations on loan restructuring. New lending instruments are policies that governments put in place to stimulate lending to the most affected economic sectors at preferential terms. Governments can stimulate SME lending from commercial banks by providing low-interest loans to banks, relaxing bank requirements and provisioning, and providing credit guarantees to lending institutions. The following provide examples:

- Armenia has provided a loan support package to SMEs in its most-affected sectors (manufacturing, transportation and storage economy, tourism, other service sectors, and health care). The loan will be provided through the Investment Support Center of the Ministry of Economy, with credit institutions acting as servicing agents for the loans. The maximum loan amount is AMD50 million, with 0% interest for the first 2 years, and 12% for the third year (Government of the Republic of Armenia 2020).
- The government of Mongolia, together with the Bank of Mongolia and commercial banks, has approved decisions to make 6-month deferrals on consumer and business loan repayment and their interest for 90 days.
- Thailand has provided B500 billion ($15 billion) in funding to commercial banks to lend to SMEs at an annual interest rate of 2% (with 0% interest for the first 6 months) (Association of Southeast Asian Nations [ASEAN] Briefing 2020a).
- The PRC encourages its financial institutions to increase tolerance for NPLs from epidemic hit sectors and MSMEs (Reuters 2020). The State Council also approved the extension of loan payment deferrals to the end of 2021.[12]

---

[12] IMF COVID-19 Policy Tracker. https://www.imf.org/en/Topics/imf-and-covid19/Policy-Responses-to-COVID-19 (accessed 15 April 2021).

⊙ Singapore has increased its risk share to 90% from 80% for loans made under the Enterprise Financing Scheme (EFS) Trade loan, EFS-SME Working Capital loan, and the Temporary Bridging Loan (ASEAN Briefing 2020b).

Additionally, policy makers have used new lending instruments to hasten digitization. Containment measures have accelerated digital transformation as social distancing and closing of markets have forced or obliged businesses to move to online platforms to continue to compete in this difficult scenario. Additionally, digital transformations and innovations are able to accelerate the role of owned and female entrepreneurs during the COVID-19 pandemic (ERIA 2020b).

⊙ Malaysia allocated RM300 million ($68 million) loans for SMEs looking to digitalize or automate their business. The financing can be used to help purchase hardware, software, and other IT solutions and services, in addition to equipment and machinery (Medina 2020).
⊙ In March 2020, the PRC government announced a package supporting the digitalization of SMEs amid COVID-19 (KPMG 2020a).
⊙ Singapore announced a S$500 million ($359 million) grant to support business digital transformation. The first measure provides S$300 per month for 5 months to stall holders in hawker centers, wet markets, coffee shops, and industrial canteens to adopt e-payment platforms and avoid handling cash. The second measure is an extension of the SMEs Go Digital program. It provides a Digital Resilience Bonus of up to S$5,000 to SMEs that adopt electronic payment and invoicing solutions, in addition to business process and e-commerce solutions (Dryer and Nygaard 2020).

To strengthen SME liquidity and ease SME cashflow problems, Asian governments have put in place tax relief measures such as rate reductions, credits, waivers, and deferrals. A total of 51 policies have been implemented for payroll, social security, value-added tax (VAT), and land taxes combined, while 50 policies for corporate tax relief exist. Examples include:

⊙ India provided a 25% rate deduction for tax deduction at source for non-salaried specified payments made to residents and rates of tax collection at source for the specified receipts (KPMG 2020b).
⊙ Fiji reduced its mandatory employee and employer contribution to the Fiji National Provident Fund (FNPF) by 5% up to 31 December 2021. Additionally, employers that contributed more than 5% will be given a 150% tax deduction (FNPF 2020).
⊙ Singapore granted an automatic deferment of income tax for companies and self-employed individuals from April to June 2020; it provided 100% property tax rebates to vulnerable business (e.g., restaurants, tourist attractions, etc.) (ASEAN Briefing 2020c).
⊙ Malaysia allowed 750,000 SMEs to postpone income tax payment for 3 months from April 2020 to June 2020 (ASEAN Briefing 2020d).
⊙ Indonesia allocated Rp123 trillion ($8.3 billion) in tax incentives, including (i) corporate income tax deduction from 25% to 20% for 2020–2021, (ii) tax relief amounting to 0.5% income tax for businesses with gross annual turnover below Rp48 billion ($326,000), and (iii) a relaxation of VAT refunds as well as deferral on import tax payments (ASEAN Briefing 2020e).
⊙ In April 2021, the PRC government announced an extension of the tax-relief policies launched in 2020 in response to the pandemic. Small-scale VAT taxpayers nationwide will continue to pay 1% VAT instead of 3% until the end of 2021 (China Briefing 2021).

Finally, due to reduced operations or outright suspension of operations, SMEs have trouble with paying workers and sick leave. This issue is particularly important as large-scale unemployment will indirectly impact the quality of household loans. Many Asian countries therefore have also prioritized employment support measures for vulnerable SME sectors. Common employment support for SMEs includes wage subsidies (37), support for informal and self-employed workers (13), labor training subsidies (8), and unemployment benefits (7).

- Georgia announced a GEL75 million ($23.55 million) informal sector and self-employed support package. The package allows informal and self-employed workers one-time assistance of GEL300 ($94.19) if they can substantiate claims of job loss (Agenda.Ge 2020).
- Bangladesh government announced a Tk50 billion stimulus package (about $595 million) for export-oriented industries. This includes assistance toward salaries and funding of 2-year loans to factory owners at 2% interest (KPMG 2020c).
- Malaysia exempted companies from paying the Human Resources Development Fund—a training fund established for skills development and retraining of employees. The government expects a RM440 million ($100 million) savings through this exemption (ASEAN Briefing 2020d).
- Singapore enhanced the Job Support Scheme by paying 75% on the first S$4,600 ($3,233) of monthly salaries for each local employee (ASEAN Briefing 2020b).
- The Republic of Korea established a W500 billion ($406 million) wage subsidy package for affected firms in all sectors keeping employees on the payroll. The package covers up to 90% of wages for SMEs (Korea Joong Ang Daily 2020).

Table 14: Top 10 Small and Medium-Sized Enterprise Support Instruments in ADB's Developing Member Countries

Total	Type of Support	Type of Instrument
77	Debt finance	New lending—under concessional terms
50	Tax	Corporate tax—rate reductions, credits, waivers, and/or deferrals
51	Tax	Payroll/social security/VAT taxes/land taxes—rate reductions, credits, waivers, and/or deferrals
42	Debt finance	Delayed repayments. Deferral of payments, restructuring, and rescheduling
37	Employment support	Provide wage subsidies (can be broad, or targeted—e.g., apprentices) as alternative to direct payments to individuals
37	Debt finance	Capital buffer safeguards requirements on banks and central banks' actions to induce commercial banks to increase lending to SMEs, such as lowering capital requirements
21	Business costs	Utilities—reduction of direct or indirect (e.g., tax concession for suppliers/landlords) fees and payments
21	Business climate	Reduced import restrictions (nontariff barriers, duties) on intermediate goods
20	Debt finance	Existing lending with reduced or no interest, and/or lower collateral requirements
19	Demand	Targeted (sector or region) expenditure programs

ADB = Asian Development Bank, SMEs = small and medium-sized enterprises, VAT = value-added tax.

Source: World Bank. Map of MSME-Support Measures in Response to COVID-19. https://www.worldbank.org/en/data/interactive/2020/04/14/map-of-sme-support-measures-in-response-to-covid-19 (accessed 9 March 2021).

Banking and Capital Markets

Looking at lessons from previous crises and what is being implemented, key crisis management solutions can be summarized into ample liquidity provisions and swift implementation of these programs (Solt 2018). An immediate and effective policy response can allow governments to stabilize financial markets and international capital flows, halt economic decline, and initiate recovery.

Recognizing the economic impact of the crisis, governments have unleashed packages of fiscal and monetary policies to maintain banking, capital, and overall financial stability, as noted. While each government has a key policy focus and features, common features implemented across Asia include increasing the liquidity of banking institutions and the capital market, through the following measures: (i) policy interest rate cuts, (ii) deregulation of reserve requirement ratios and other regulatory ratios for financial institutions, (iii) central bank liquidity injections, (iv) regulatory forbearance to free up bank liquidity, (v) broadening eligible collateral for repo transactions as liquidity support, and (vi) outright purchases of government bonds and corporate bonds and securities. Table 15 shows the total package by measure in selected Asian economies. A detailed policy response summary is also illustrated in the Appendix.

Table 15: Total Package by Measure in Select Asian Economies
($ million)

Economy/Measure	Liquidity Support ($ million)	Credit Creation ($ million)	Direct Long-Term Lending ($ million)	Equity Support ($ million)
Central and West Asia				
Armenia	n.a.	51	n.a.	0
Kazakhstan	4,245	n.a	873	0
East Asia				
China, People's Republic of	427,468	445,065	50,871	28,498
Hong Kong, China	129,786	9,066	n.a.	2,511
Korea, Republic of	17,745	3,115	113,844	9,426
Mongolia	245	126	966	0
South Asia				
Bangladesh	4,473	4,356	589	5,035
India	159,042	63,981	n.a.	0
Sri Lanka	n.a.	811	n.a.	450
Pacific				
Fiji	n.a.	27	45	0
Vanuatu	n.a.	n.a	13	0

continued on next page

Table 15 *continued*

Economy/Measure	Liquidity Support ($ million)	Credit Creation ($ million)	Direct Long-Term Lending ($ million)	Equity Support ($ million)
Southeast Asia				
Indonesia	14,638	16,453	45,753	559
Malaysia	17,680	11,872	26,572	279
Philippines	7,345	2,456	2,204	18,318
Thailand	n.a.	34,260	17,130	0

n.a. = not available/no amount

Source: Asian Development Bank. ADB COVID-19 Policy Database, https://covid19policy.adb.org/policy-measures (accessed 23 June 2021).

Insurance and Pensions

The policy and regulatory response to COVID-19 has primarily focused on operational relief and resilience of insurers, with prudential measures aimed at capital preservation, enhanced risk management and reporting, and with conduct of business measures to ensure fair treatment of customers.

These responses have included the following:

- Grace periods on insurance premium payment.
- Deferred payment or temporary reductions of social security contributions. These measures are introduced to reduce labor costs directly borne by employers, keeping companies from going out of business, and allowing them to retain their workers in paid employment.
- Exempting conduct requirements (such as face-to-face explanation) to reduce the risk to intermediaries and their clients.
- Monitoring timely handling and payment of claims are important to keep public confidence in the insurance industry.
- Requiring health insurers to cover COVID-19 testing without copayment by the policyholder. However, universal insurance coverage is inadequate for informal workers in terms of out-of-pocket expenditure, availability, accessibility of services, quality, and financial sustainability.
- The governments of Bangladesh, India, Indonesia, and Nepal have provided life and health insurance coverage to frontline health workers, including sanitation staff, paramedics, nurses, and community health workers.
- Relaxing nonessential reporting and other requirements to facilitate business continuity of insurers.
- Premium loans against policy cash value or after conversion to a paid-up policy by reducing the sum assured.
- Social pension advances to senior citizens, widows, and people with disabilities.

Insurance industry response

Innovative health insurance products. Many examples of innovative solutions in the health insurance segment have emerged in the insurance market since the COVID-19 pandemic began to offset the infection's impact. Some insurance companies are now offering a discount by providing 1 month free coverage (i.e., 13 months of coverage for the price of 12). In some countries, such as India[13] and Singapore,[14] this is driven by insurance regulation; in other markets, e.g., the Philippines,[15] this is through the goodwill of insurers.

Lines of credit to MSMEs. In partnership with banks, insurers are offering lines of credit to MSMEs that purchase their products and provide online education about more complex financial products. For example, in Thailand, besides offering low interest loans, Siam Commercial Bank is offering a special COVID-19 insurance package to SME owners.[16]

Support insurance agents and intermediaries in their COVID-19 response. Insurance agents and intermediaries are often the first point of interface for customers when they need to purchase a new insurance policy or file a claim. Prioritizing support for agents not only has helped them cope with COVID-19 but has also ensured that their customers receive good support. The use of digital tools has enabled insurance sales without face-to-face contact with clients.

Corporate social responsibility. Insurers have made donations to COVID-19 initiatives, and some have encouraged customers and the public to donate. For example, in the Philippines, InLife launched a public crowdfunding campaign with donations from employees, agents, and partners, and peso-for-peso matching from the Insular Foundation. The funds received have been used to buy personal protective equipment for medical workers, kitchen equipment, and food for the temporary shelters housing frontline medical workers, and food packages for economically distressed communities.

ADB's response to the crisis

ADB has been providing technical assistance to its developing member countries (DMCs) and partnering with other development organizations to help developing Asia battle the pandemic. ADB is also working on bringing public and private sectors together to forge innovative solutions. It has approved grants under the Asia Pacific Disaster Response Fund grants, and various nonsovereign operations, for immediate and rapid response.

Under the overall lead of respective governments, ADB is closely coordinating with key development partners, including on cofinancing. It is coordinating with the governments of Cambodia, Indonesia, the Philippines, and Thailand on possible cofinancing of the COVID-19 Active Response and Expenditure Support Program (CARES). To date, ADB has committed to cofinancing with the Asian Infrastructure Investment Bank, Japan International Cooperation Agency, KfW, and the Agence Française de Développement. In August 2020, ADB CARES agreed to provide a quick-disbursing $1.5 billion loan to support the Government of Thailand's response to COVID-19 (Biospectrum 2020). ADB cofinanced with the PRC-led Asian Infrastructure Investment Bank to extend $750 million in loans and Japan International Cooperation Agency ($460 million) to support the Philippine

---

13 In India, Bharti AXA General Insurance has partnered with Airtel Payments Bank to offer two types of affordable health insurance plans that target individuals as well as groups. The individual plan offers a lump sum benefit, while the group plan provides a fixed daily hospital allowance.

14 In Singapore, DBS Bank, in partnership with CHUBB Insurance, offered a free COVID-19 hospital cash benefit to the bank's customers that will pay for hospitalization due to the virus.

15 In the Philippines, FWD Insurance added a medical benefit for life insurance policyholders diagnosed with COVID-19, as well as extra cover for funeral costs if the policyholder dies from the virus.

16 For information, see the Siam Commercial Bank company website at https://www.scb.co.th/en/about-us/news/mar-2020/support-sme-covide-19.html.

government's efforts to combat COVID-19 and mitigate its adverse impact on the economy (de Vera 2020). In September 2020, ADB and KfW, a German state-owned development bank, signed agreements for about $525 million in cofinancing to enhance Indonesia's COVID-19 response and improve financial inclusion in the country (ADB 2020e). Cambodia and ADB, cofinanced by the Agence Française de Développement, agreed to a $250 million concessional loan and a linked package of technical assistance with advisory support for COVID-19 response. Grants and technical assistance resources are being mobilized through direct support or ADB-administered trust funds or with contributions from Australia's Department of Foreign Affairs and Trade and the Nordic Development Fund, as well as France, Japan, the Republic of Korea, and others. ADB has also collaborated with the United Nations Children's Fund to facilitate the procurement of Asia Pacific Disaster Response Fund-financed emergency medical supplies and equipment in the Lao People's Democratic Republic (ADB n.d.).

Since the onset of the crisis, ADB's Trade and Supply Chain Finance Programs have supported 864 transactions in Viet Nam valued at $550 million and 55 medical and pharmaceutical transactions in Malaysia valued at $15 million. In Indonesia, ADB is experimenting on providing nonsovereign support to businesses critical in ensuring food security and communications, and important in the current socioeconomic crisis. In the Philippines, ADB has been supporting the public–private "Task Force T3" (test, trace, and treat) to support the rapid and expanded testing project of the government.

The bank has continuously extended emergency assistance lending and appropriate solutions to mitigate the effects of the health crisis. In March 2020, ADB announced a package amounting to $6.5 billion to help DMCs respond to COVID-19. In particular, the package is dedicated to respond to the health and economic consequences of the pandemic in sovereign and nonsovereign operations. ADB plans to expand the financing up to $13 billion to fund countercyclical expenditures, and additional grant and technical assistance resources. In April 2020, ADB announced to triple the response package to $20 billion and established a COVID-19 Pandemic Response Option under ADB's Countercyclical Support Facility to further streamline its operations for quicker and more flexible delivery of assistance to severely affected DMCs. In November 2020, ADB launched a $9 billion vaccine initiative, the Asia Pacific Vaccine Access Facility, to provide a comprehensive program to support DMCs' vaccine process. The funding will be complemented with special policy variations and response measures to directly address the economic impacts emanating from the losses brought about by the pandemic. By the end of 2020, ADB was able to provide resources to 41 member countries in the form of loans, grants, and technical assistance. To address the impacts of COVID-19, India, Indonesia, Kazakhstan, the Philippines, and Thailand each received more than $1 billion in commitments. As of 21 June 2021, ADB's total committed amount has reached $18.54 billion (ADB 2021). Table 16 documents the bank's expanded response package to about $20 billion for 202 projects. These resources will go hand-in-hand with special policy variations and response measures to enable ADB to implement a swift and comprehensive approach to support DMCs' responses to the global health issue (ADB 2020f).

**Table 16: Available Asian Development Bank Resources for COVID-19 Response,
as of 21 June 2021**

($ billion)

| Item | Commitments | | | |
	ADB	Cofinancing	Commercial Cofinancing	Total
Sovereign	**13.620**	**8.599**	**0.000**	**22.219**
Grant	0.480	0.029		0.509
Loan	13.000	8.550		21.55
Technical assistance	0.140	0.020		0.160
Nonsovereign	**4.405**	**0.001**	**5.196**	**9.602**
Guarantee	3.600		4.780	8.380
Loan	0.650		0.400	1.050
Debt security	0.150		0.016	0.166
Technical assistance	0.005	0.001		0.006
Total	**18.025**	**8.600**	**5.196**	**31.821**

Source: Asian Development Bank. COVID-19 (Coronavirus): ADB's Response. https://www.adb.org/what-we-do/covid19-coronavirus (accessed 25 June 2021).

ADB projects originally planned for 2020, meanwhile, have been utilized to help people and economies in the region to bounce back from the pandemic. Indonesia's policy-based loan totaling $1 billion programmed to promote innovative financial inclusion, competitive industrial modernization, and sustainable and inclusive energy access, for example, could be used for critical financing needs related to the health crisis. In the Philippines, some funds of the policy-based lending program to support competitive agriculture development and inclusive finance development and the social assistance program could be utilized as direct support to the country's budget and general economic stimulus. ADB has also reprogrammed $375 million in project funds in the agriculture and natural resources sector to consider COVID-19 impacts. Similarly, ADB adjusted arrangements in the transport sector to reflect the "new normal" by adding prevention measures in construction sites, strengthening monitoring, and reviewing system designs to minimize risk exposure to infectious diseases (ADB n.d.).

4 Policy Considerations for Stability and Resilience Post-COVID-19

The immediate policies and measures detailed in the previous section have been crucial in mitigating the impacts of the pandemic. But these have enabled the buildup of financial imbalances and vulnerabilities such as unsustainable debt and reduced credit quality, which would likely threaten long-term financial stability. Moreover, pandemic challenges including virus mutations and divergent growth across economies continue to pose risks, making regional economic prospects and financial conditions uncertain. Policy makers should therefore seek to pursue the "New Normal 2.0" policy considerations focused on strengthening financial stability, resilience, and development in the post-COVID-19 period. This can lead to more effective crisis response and stronger growth opportunities. This section details important measures that can aid policy makers in the post-COVID-19 period.

Establishing a Financial Framework for Epidemic Risk Financing

COVID-19, as a highly contagious disease, presents new challenges and risks to national emergency, health, and fiscal systems. In particular, as noted earlier, household consumption and economic growth in developing countries across Asia and the Pacific are hampered due to plunging tourist revenues and slowing trade and production.

However, developing countries, including in Asia and the Pacific, remain unprepared for disease outbreaks, given severe health sector shortcomings and financing gaps. Filling these gaps is crucial to help prevent disease outbreaks from becoming more deadly and costly pandemics. A regional institution taking on a coordinating and supportive role across the region's countries is required to prepare response capacity to local and national outbreaks, before they spread regionally, by linking and coordinating countries with regional surveillance networks based on international standards. This takes account of the wide disparity of the countries' current health security.

Theories on effective regional public goods call for weaker/weakest-link aggregation technology (ADB 2018). Weak institutions and low technical capacity among developing countries in the region can impede national and regional efforts to contain a virus. Multilateral development banks can therefore provide invaluable support to regional public goods provision. ADB, with its strong regional presence and commitment to health and economic stability, is well positioned to support efforts to strengthen health security across its DMCs.

ADB suggests filling financial and technical gaps through a regional Epidemic Risk Financing framework (ADB n.d.). The framework could help identify the critical financing gap arising from lack of national funds or financing instruments (Tables 17 and 18). ADB could support DMCs by (i) increasing the financial response capacity of national and subnational governments to meet post-disaster funding needs without compromising fiscal balances and development objectives; (ii) strengthening governments' ability to implement policy measures for creating an enabling environment for private market development that contributes to greater financial resilience against disasters; (iii) building the capacity of governments for informed decisions on disaster risk finance, based on sound financial/actuarial analysis; and (iv) providing information that will lead to informed actions for building financial resilience. Additionally, the framework would complement existing financial safety nets provided by the IMF Catastrophe Containment and Relief Trust and the World Bank's planned Health Emergency Preparedness and Response Multi-Donor Fund.[17] It could also provide specific ADB funds for immediate emergency response. Based on lessons learned, ADB Epidemic Risk Financing could seek to accomplish the following:

- Tailor fit the scope of pathogens to the infectious disease profile of the region.
- Make criteria and threshold for payouts easily accessible and timely.
- Cover ADB DMCs, including those in the World Bank Group's International Development Association and ineligible DMCs,[18] including pay-out triggers based on rigorous assessment using pandemic risk models for epidemic outbreaks before they become pandemics.
- Respond to immediate financial needs to implement containment and mitigation strategies and support affected economic sectors, including the most vulnerable populations and MSMEs.
- Make critical infrastructure more resilient.
- Explore diverse risk financing tools including risk transfer solutions such as cash, loans, bonds, pandemic catastrophe bonds and other insurance-linked securities, traditional insurance and reinsurance products.
- Promote the economic benefits of risk transfer solutions through government subsidies as well as through the establishment of public-private loss-sharing infectious disease insurance pool programs to protect consumers, businesses, and subnational governments.
- Provide capacity building and training and bridge risk modeling experts and the insurance and capital markets for designing tailor-made risk financing decisions.

---

[17] The World Bank Pandemic Emergency Facility. https://www.worldbank.org/en/news/press-release/2020/04/27/pef-allocates-us195-million-to-more-than-60-low-income-countries-to-fight-covid-19, has not been renewed and is being replaced by the Health Emergency Preparedness and Response Muliti-Donor Fund; see https://www.worldbank.org/en/news/statement/2020/04/15/world-bank-group-to-launch-new-multi-donor-trust-fund-to-help-countries-prepare-for-disease-outbreaks.

[18] Eligibility for International Development Association support depends first and foremost on a country's relative poverty, defined as gross national income per capita below an established threshold and updated annually ($1,175 in fiscal year 2020): 76 countries are currently eligible to receive some form of International Development Association resources (see https://ida.worldbank.org/about/borrowing-countries for more information).

ADB could also consider a policy discussion forum to strengthen national technical and financial capacity. This could enhance regional health security as a regional public good. This forum could evolve into a regional epidemic disease risk prevention and control center.

Table 17: Key Elements of an Epidemic Risk Financing Framework at the Country Level

Public Health Infrastructure	Surveillance
	Immunization
	Medical workforce
	Hospital capacity
	Coordination
Physical Infrastructure	Water and sanitation
	Roads
	Phones
	Internet
	Logistics
Institutional Capacity	Political stability
	Corruption
	Bureaucratic effectiveness
	Armed conflict
	Homicide
	Vital registration
	Risk analysis and data
Financial Resources	Health sector budget (% of gross domestic product)
	Per capita income
	Out-of-pocket health spending
	Resource dependency
	Health insurance
Public Health Communication	Public awareness
	Risk communication

Source: Lee, Kessler, and Chatterjee (2020).

Table 18: Key Elements of Regional Epidemic Risk Financing Framework

Countries	Government, Industry, and Academia	Risks	Ministries of Finance, Central Banks and Financial Regulators, Banks and Financial Institutions	International Organizations and Businesses	Universities and Specialized Training Organizations
Ability to prevent, detect, and respond to outbreaks	Access to vaccines and medical countermeasures	Understanding and communicating risks	Contingent Financing, Loans, Risk sharing and risk transfer	WHO/UN/OIE/ coordination and response	Skills to communicate and manage outbreaks
↑	↑	↑	↑	↑	↑
Strengthening public health core capacity	Improving access to technology and data	Reinforcing, data collections, risk analysis, and incentives for action	Strengthening financial resilience and financial stability	Strengthening global mechanisms	Enhancing awareness, capacity building, and training

Regional Cooperation and Coordination Platform
(Country representatives, development partners, research institutions, experts, practitioners, data scientists, financial industry representatives)

OIE = World Organisation for Animal Health, UN = United Nations, WHO = World Health Organization.

Source: Lee, J., T. Kessler, and A. Chatterjee. 2020. Note on the Asian Development Bank Epidemic Risk Financing Framework for Asian Developing Countries.

For Asia and the Pacific to fight outbreaks requires meticulous preparation and rapid response starting at the country level. National public health infrastructure must be sustainable and have resilient capacities to prevent, detect, and respond to large-scale epidemics. Then, with the help of regional cooperation and coordination in the region, economies can prevent most epidemic outbreaks from spreading regionally and internationally after transforming into pandemics. In addition, the countries in the region can limit the impacts to their national economies.

Buttressing Financial Stability and Macroprudential Policies

Over a year after the first recorded case of COVID-19, the pandemic has severely hampered global economic activity and loomed over financial stability. The emerging market and developing economies have faced sharp, unexpected capital outflows and remain exposed to international spillovers through various channels. These show that financial stability and macroprudential policies are an important complement to the unprecedented fiscal, monetary, and emergency liquidity actions taken to offset the painful economic effects of COVID-19. It is now paramount to closely monitor the resilience of financial systems critical for financial services and financial stability.

A.   Short-term (6 months–1 year)

Challenges and issues

The impact of the COVID-19 shock has also extended to supply as health precautions and illnesses have disrupted production among businesses. As noted in Chapter 2, the virus spread easily in close contact and authorities implemented social distancing measures, forcing companies to operate with skeletal workforces. These limited operations, slowing delivery of goods and services. Labor supply declined as the number of sick workers rose and lockdowns and quarantines saw capacity utilization drop.

As noted earlier, the pandemic also triggered a severe demand shock that interrupted cash flows and upset payment systems. Millions of people and counting have lost their jobs and incomes, raising uncertainty, reducing global spending, and exacerbating a contraction in demand. Commodity exporters, emerging markets, developing economies highly dependent on tourism, and receivers of remittances have faced large negative shocks. As consumer and business sentiment has worsened, many firms have reduced their investment in economies (IMF 2020b).

The global health crisis also affected the liquidity of economies. A sudden downturn in investor sentiment and flight to safety tightened financial conditions globally and, as noted, countries faced significant outflow pressures and reserve losses. This has burdened exchange rates and credit spreads of emerging market and developing economies and the likelihood of credit defaults, financial distress, and macroeconomic instability has increased (IMF 2020b).

Financial, monetary, and supervisory measures

A relaxation of selected macroprudential tools can help financial systems absorb shocks, particularly shocks like the COVID-19 pandemic. However, it is only possible if countries have existing macroprudential buffers and only useful if the buffers are expected to relieve stress or remove binding constraints on the provision of credit to real economies (IMF 2014, 2017). Central bank monetary measures such as cutting policy rates, will increase investment and income, which may help avoid a credit crunch and support economic demand. This must push commercial banks to lend to households and firms where the cash-flow process is disrupted.

Authorities can also consider temporarily easing financial regulations and supervisory standards so that financial institutions can expand their capacity to supply funds to the real sector in times of crisis with clear indication of expiry or "time limits" of such measures. Additional considerations can be given to readjust capital requirements for financial institutions by easing their standards of asset classification. Specifically, measures exist to reduce the burden on financial institutions by reducing the frequency of inspections, extending deadlines for submitting reports, and reducing the number of inspection-related tests.

Prudential measures

Financial authorities can also implement several extraordinary measures through regulatory forbearance: (i) freezing the classification status of all credit exposures before the pandemic, (ii) extending the number of past-due days after which credit is considered nonperforming, and (iii) allowing banks to postpone adequate provisioning for loans covered by moratoriums. Forbearance in classifying the quality of loans could cause lasting damage to transparency, however, as such measures also cover actual losses and the true financial position of a bank (IMF and World Bank 2020).

Some countries (Indonesia and Malaysia) in Southeast Asia and elsewhere in East Asia and the Pacific, have at times relaxed regulatory capital buffers to support the flow of credit to the economy (World Bank 2020a). This will boost the capacity of financial institutions to lend through periods of increased credit risk. However, the temporary easing of the relevant capital requirements or buffers may act against the business cycle and can be inefficient and counterproductive in economic downturns, as little evidence in the literature proves its effectiveness in slowing credit growth (Basel Committee on Banking Supervision 2018).

To counter liquidity stress in local currency, banks may use their high-quality liquidity assets under the liquidity coverage ratio and relax reserve requirements. In addition, foreign currency reserve requirements can be lowered to mitigate pressures in foreign currency funding (IMF 2020b).

Lowering sectoral tools such as caps on loan-to-value ratios will also be useful in supporting credit provision to households and firms.

- Open market operations
  » To provide additional liquidity to financial systems, central banks rapidly purchased private and public bonds and commercial paper to buy time for taming the epidemic and to avoid financial meltdown. As "buyers of last resort" in these markets, the central banks are able to mitigate upward pressures on the credit cost while ensuring that both households and firms have affordable access to credit (Adrian and Natalucci 2020).

- International cooperation
  » A number of central banks have also agreed to enhance the provision of US dollar liquidity through swap line arrangements with special attention to Asia's developing countries, where blockage of global trade, foreign currency-denominated debt, and sudden capital outflows threaten to cause economic devastation. The currency swap lines, as well as IMF's rapid financing instruments (short-term liquidity line), were highly instrumental in stabilizing emerging market and developing economies. These swap lines work well, with the help of policy advice and capacity development (IMF 2020b).

Fiscal policy measures

As of 11 September, fiscal measures announced globally amounted to $11.7 trillion. Half of the budget went to additional spending or forgone revenue, including temporary tax cuts, and the other half was allocated to liquidity support, including loans, guarantees, and equity injections by the public sector. The size and composition of fiscal support depends on the countries' available fiscal space. Non-health fiscal measures include: (i) cash and in-kind transfers to those most in need, (ii) wage subsidies for furloughed workers or businesses with revenue losses, (iii) loans and guarantees through public corporations, (iv) equity injections to hard-hit strategic firms, (v) tax payment deferral and extension, and (vi) payment forbearance policies. Given that resources are limited, the bulk of the fiscal support should be geared toward safeguarding enhanced social safety nets and helping viable but still vulnerable firms to reopen after business interruptions. However, governments may consider providing guarantees on relevant parts of loans to overcome liquidity needs of cash-strapped businesses, if their budgets allow the appropriate amounts (IMF 2020d). Debt moratoriums and large-scale fiscal support, including credit guarantees, have provided relief to affected households and SMEs. Although this may have stretched fiscal space and strengthened the bank-sovereign nexus in some countries, liquidity buffers in domestic and foreign currency should also be used, if needed, in compliance with the standard or other liquidity requirements. These measures should maintain support to affected borrowers, promote balance sheet transparency, and ensure continuity and operations of businesses and payment systems (IMF and World Bank 2020).

B.   Medium-term (2–3 years)

Challenges and issues

The uncertainty associated with the crisis will drag on investment, consumption, and growth. Unemployment and firm closures will have created mismatches and disorientation in normal resource allocation. Investors are concerned about profitability and prospects for economies in the wake of the pandemic. Prolonged deterioration in investment sentiment can therefore have serious implications for economies, especially if the economies depend heavily on foreign direct investments. In consumption and economic growth, pandemic mitigation measures have hindered consumption of goods and services, requiring close human interaction. This includes, as noted, restrictions on movement of individuals and the operations of services such as mass transport, domestic tourism, restaurants, and recreational activities (movie theaters, parks, etc.) to contain the spread of the virus, with all of the adverse economic consequences noted earlier. These restrictions can undermine economic growth and sustainability and contribute to mass closure of businesses and unemployment (World Bank 2020a). Until COVID-19 vaccines are widely distributed, the virus will continue to drive hundreds of millions back into poverty and worsen the livelihood of billions as lockdowns and quarantines financially hurt the poor and the vulnerable in Asia's developing countries.

High inflation due to overabundance of money and credit, as noted, coupled with planned fiscal expansions and the persistence of negative supply shocks, is also a concern. Inflation in many emerging markets and developing economies may remain above central bank targets, which will further constrain monetary policy stances, as bond market activity in late February 2021 has suggested.

World indebtedness is likely already increasing and includes higher levels of private and public cross-border debts. The pandemic has induced high levels of public debt on low- and middle-income countries, as these countries struggle to finance public health, social, and economic responses to the crisis. Debt will likely accumulate amid low remittances and ripple effects on domestic finance. Debt defaults are rising and putting pressure on banking systems (OECD 2020d).

Measures

Monetary and prudential policies must act jointly, and their main preoccupation must be financial stability to dampen the impact of global financial shocks on economic activity in emerging markets and developing economies. Sound and well-coordinated monetary and prudential policy measures must continue to support real economies while preserving financial stability. In implementing measures, however, domestic minimum prudential standards and internationally agreed standards must be upheld to ensure trust and confidence in the banking sector. This will also sustain the stability of financial systems and the soundness of financial institutions (IMF and World Bank 2020).

Central banks must coordinate with fiscal authorities, providing technical and quantitative support to the financing of their policies. Major multilateral agencies such as ADB, the IMF, the United Nations, and World Health Organization provide rich documentation of their technical guidance and notes on public health management.

Fiscal policies should continue to include redistributive measures, debt-financed public expenditures, transfers, and tax relief. Specifically, these targeted fiscal measures often include cash transfers, wage subsidies, credit guarantees, unemployment benefits, and tax deferrals (IMF 2020b). In Georgia, one fiscal measure is a moratorium on tax payments for low-income earners. Azerbaijan has approved tax payment deferrals. The PRC included tax breaks and deferrals in its fiscal stimulus package (World Bank 2020a). In addition, increases in public debt should in part substitute unsustainable private debts, helping firms and households to deleverage and reconstruct the capital stock eaten up by the COVID-19 shock and its consequences.

Monetary policy must help the placement of new public debt, monitor banks' liquidity, keep interest rates credibly low, and neutralize speculative and distortive shapes in their term structure, as well as excessive spreads between interest rates and debtors. Likewise, central banks need to provide funding to market segments where monetary transmission has become impaired.

Macro and microprudential measures should aim at preserving financial stability and sustainability in a period of major increases in public debt and speedy restructuring of private firms and finance. In addition, in supporting prudent restructuring, banks are encouraged by supervisors to implement enhanced credit monitoring approaches and specific public disclosure agreements. Through these, credit is being well monitored at the micro and macroprudential levels. Monetary stability becomes a component of financial stability, much more than usual (IMF and World Bank 2020).

Macroprudential tools should not be conceived as emergency means to check exaggerations in the monetary financing of public deficits: they should be actively used to reinforce the otherwise insufficient impact of purely monetary techniques. These tools should safeguard financial stability and complement changes made to improve monetary policy effectiveness.

"Super low interest rates forever" must be discouraged, the size of central bank balance sheets must find a limit, and excessive flattening of risk premiums must be avoided to defend financial markets' efficiency in allocating resources.

C.   Long term

Challenges and issues

Financial stability is a controversial exercise and can sometimes require monetary policies that do not favor price stability. This will be counterintuitive as monetary policies should address price stability, control inflation, and make public finances sound.

However, financial stability depends heavily on factors far from being controlled by monetary authorities. Central banks and supervisory authorities should also look closely at financial system resilience. In particular, authorities should monitor nodes critical for financial stability. Weaknesses and interactions in these nodes could tighten financial conditions and affect financial services provision, monetary policy execution and transmission, and possibly financial system stability (IMF and World Bank 2020).

Financial stability issues are often heavily politicized and could endanger the independence of monetary policy. The finance sector policy responses need to be well-coordinated and communicated among different line ministries in the government to contribute to the financial system's ability to finance the macroeconomy and minimize fragmentation risks and cross-border contagion. However, central banks must be left independent to improve monetary policy efficiency (IMF and World Bank 2020).

Measures

As such, financial stability should be explicitly included in monetary policy targets and monetary and prudential policies must be continuously coordinated. When monetary policy is used to improve financial stability, the result would generate positive but only moderate gains, which are partly offset by costs associated with an increase in the variability of inflation (Van der Ghote 2019). The mandate of monetary policy should include macrofinancial stability, not just price stability. On the other hand, the coordination between monetary and macroprudential policies contribute to (i) decreasing the hazards of an incoming financial crisis, and (ii) assisting in a swift exit (Van der Ghote 2018).

Financial fragilities will gradually become a dominant theme and plans to reduce leverage in the long term must be prepared in a timely manner and preannounced as part of internationally coordinated action. The pandemic has deeply strained large-scale capital outflows, which may have persistent effects on economies. Given that COVID-19 is a global shock, the effectiveness of some policies and measures could possibly be strengthened or diminished if several countries implemented them simultaneously (IMF 2020b). Thus, economies should build on efforts to coordinate an international response to uncertainties brought about by the outbreak.

International multilateral cooperation must be very active and creative in most of the policy reactions to the COVID-19 shock. Strategic partnerships of multilateral organizations must be established to encourage sharing of information and strengthen alignment with global approaches to resolution of the pandemic.

As the pandemic passes, gradual increases in interest rates will have to be targeted by monetary policies while assuring good liquidity conditions for bank lending. Ensuring that liquidity levels have been restored will prevent additional stress on banks and on financial systems. Moreover, prudential regulation should, in the meantime, increase the minimum capital adequacy ratio and decrease the maximum leverage ratio of banks, also manage exposure limits by industry and sector. Coherent fiscal measures should be decided to gradually reduce public debt and long overdue reform should invert tax incentives of debt versus equity financing.

Dangerous, stressing periods during this deleveraging phase should be carefully monitored. Deleveraging should be assisted by an ease of liquidity conditions and prudential constraints. A number of authorities have temporarily allowed their liquidity coverage ratios to drop below the minimum requirement and have supported banks in deploying their stock of high-quality liquid assets. Relaxing borrower-based macroprudential constraints is an additional measure to support lending (IMF and World Bank 2020).

Supporting international and regional cooperation

Regular sharing of information among financial authorities on evolving financial stability threats, on the policy measures that the authorities are taking or are considering, and on the effects of those policies should be encouraged. Promoting international coordination and standardizing approaches would be beneficial to countries with limited policy capacity. International cooperation will help the said countries in appropriate policy making (IMF and World Bank 2020).

Assessment is needed of potential vulnerabilities to better understand the impacts of COVID-19 on financial markets in individual jurisdictions and across the region, and these should inform discussions of policy issues. Regional vulnerabilities to health and economic stress during outbreaks disrupt financial market activities. The magnitude of these disruptions varies by country as factors like the gravity of the domestic outbreak, the vulnerability of the economy to global economic and financial stress spillovers, stark challenges in poverty and economic informality, and debt levels also constrain the fiscal response (World Bank 2020a). Government and domestic and regional supervisors must therefore coordinate policy responses to address the financial stability implications of COVID-19.

Such coordination needs to include the measures of standard-setting bodies and national authorities that provide flexibility within international standards or reduce operational burdens. Specifically, guidance and notes to support efforts by national authorities can help provide additional operational capacity to respond to immediate financial stability priorities. Likewise, the use of the flexibility existing within international standards can be promoted in the international financial community (IMF and World Bank 2020). These actions will provide rapid and coordinated policy responses.

Developing Insurance Markets for Risk Sharing and Transfer Solutions

The current global health crisis forced manufacturing plants, restaurants, retail establishments, and other places of business to operate with skeletal workforces or halt operations to limit the spread of COVID-19. SMEs are notably and highly vulnerable to disasters due to natural hazards and to pandemics. Low investment by SMEs in disaster resilience and business interruption insurance exposes them to destruction of property and equipment, damage to stock, revenue loss, and rising operational costs. Moreover, these businesses may lose market share as customers shift to competitors, skilled workers move, and retailers and suppliers impair their relationships, which affect their long-term sustainability (Chatterjee 2020). As a result, policyholders can accrue significant business interruption losses unless governments (or courts) intervene. Policy makers need to examine longer-term solutions to address gaps in financial protection for business interruption related to pandemics and natural hazards.

For now, however, insurers and their associations say most policyholders lack insurance coverage to respond to business interruption losses of the pandemic. This absence is expected to lead to significant arguments between insurers and their policyholders over the coming months (if not years). Proposals to require insurers to pay claims for losses that they did not intend to cover and for which they have not collected premiums or set aside provisions/reserves could have serious implications. The scale of losses that policyholders are incurring due to business disruption are multiples of the amount that insurers will normally payout for business interruption claims. Insurance supervisors are also concerned about the implications of retroactively expanding coverage obligations for the solvency of insurance companies (OECD 2020c).

At any rate, SMEs themselves need to manage risks and internal processes meticulously by integrating catastrophe risk insurance into their business operations and decision-making processes. They need to assess the risk of a business unit's "threat landscape, the financial impact, and the recovery time to properly target those risks and challenges in a catastrophe. Business must also reasonably quantify actual losses in terms of average cost of construction and time to rebuild. They must also evaluate ongoing contractual arrangements or exposures to third parties that will continue regardless of whether the business is closed or open. A robust cost–benefit analysis of potential risk mitigation options based on the frequency and severity of the impact of the disaster is also required. In addition, businesses should explore risk- and cost-sharing arrangements for liability exposures, besides governmental emergency funds or other financing sources to cover for losses. After an informed assessment to determine the amount of risk they can retain, the amount of premium they can afford to pay for risk transfer via insurance, and the amount of deductible, companies can purchase business interruption insurance (Chatterjee 2020).

Given the unique nature of business interruption due to COVID-19, specialized coverage for insurance is needed. In many jurisdictions, coverage is limited to physical damage, and contamination due to viruses may not be considered damage to property and equipment. The cost of coverage may also be substantial as the magnitude of business interruption losses as a result of the pandemic is much higher than the losses incurred as a result of a single catastrophic event. Generally, it is a challenge to include coverage for pandemic risk, although it has been available, businesses have not frequently acquired it in purchasing business interruption insurance (OECD 2020c). As noted, COVID-19 has severely hampered all parts of the world, but diversifying exposure in the financial market geographically will be limited. Thus, little risk reduction coverage may be available.

The nature of a pandemic requires the specific design of a pandemic risk insurance program to achieve broad coverage, limit public sector exposure, and encourage risk reduction. First, governments may consider approaches that automatically extend insurance coverage for pandemic risk to ensure broader coverage. Doing so would void relevant exclusions to coverage under specific circumstances, such as losses due to a pandemic. An *optional* basis coverage for targeted perils will have more limited success in reducing the business interruption protection gap. Second, the design of the program must assess the appetite of the private insurance market to provide coverage for pandemic outbreak scenarios. Government-backing as a reinsurer of last resort should target the highest layer of losses so that private insurance markets can develop their limits for threshold losses lower than the government's target limit. As it may take time before private insurance markets will be willing to make available significant capacity, the threshold limits for government involvement may need to be set at fairly low levels. Lastly, insurers could be required to ensure that policyholders have business continuity plans or other risk mitigation measures in place relevant to a pandemic. Such measures could allow continuity of operations (by implementing work-from-home arrangements) and reduce business interruption losses incurred during widespread business closures (OECD 2020c).

In emerging Asia, 85% of small businesses do not fully comprehend the risk of natural catastrophes for managing business continuity. Less than 15% of those who have flood insurance have purchased business interruption coverage. Risk management and insurance is their lowest priority, leaving small businesses vulnerable to unforeseen financial losses arising from natural hazards.

Yet, business interruption coverage can be made accessible and affordable to small businesses. First, the businesses could establish cooperative arrangements akin to a risk pool where they can contribute in proportion to the risk on their books. This arrangement would allow better negotiation of insurance premiums. Second, insurers should use financial technology to assist in underwriting, detect underinsurance, and assess business interruption claims. Fintech provides alternative risk scoring metrics based on the volume of cashflow by using e-commerce payment platforms, digital wallets, and mobile financial services. This will help insurers widen their reach. Finally, parametric insurance solutions using big data, artificial intelligence, and machine-learning technology should be designed to enable immediate payment of claims while reducing administration costs, investigation, and reserving questions (Chatterjee 2020).

Business interruption insurance, essential to the business continuity toolkit, should be promoted through financial literacy programs. SMEs need to continue doing business even amid the severe interruptions of a pandemic. Yet the appetite of private insurance markets to ensure pandemic risk is limited. Catastrophe models for pandemic risk focused on business interruption losses should therefore be carefully designed to include a pandemic risk business interruption program.

Improving SME Financing

Among COVID-19 impacts, on the demand side, the economic slowdown has reduced income, minimizing expenditure on goods and services due to the fear of contagion and heightened uncertainty. Workers have been laid off with firms unable to pay them. On the supply side, staff have been unable to report to work and lockdowns and quarantines have cut into sales, markets, and supply chains, seriously impairing business operations. The perceived risks of lending to the sector have increased in response, even as accessing finance becomes more paramount to mitigate the impact of the pandemic and enable long-term SMEs to recover.

The initial impact of the pandemic on small businesses has been abrupt, as indicated in results from a 31 March to 6 April 2020 survey of impact on SMEs in the region conducted by the Asia–Pacific MSME Trade Coalition. The group identifies five major challenges for MSMEs (Figure 12). About 50% of SMEs surveyed said they only had a month, or just less, of cash reserves. Restrictions on movement and containment measures had reduced consumer demand and caused business closures, they said. Lockdown policies hampered manufacturing, logistics, and shipping of products as workers were unable to return to work and restore production processes. Opportunities to meet new clients were reduced as the state advised firms and households to stay and work from home. SMEs struggled to change business models and strategies and provide new products or services in high demand (Vandenberg 2020).

Figure 12: Key Challenges for Micro, Small, and Medium-Sized Enterprises

1. Lack of operational cash flow

2. Drop in demand for products and services

3. Business is closed
   CLOSE

4. Reduction of opportunities to meet new clients

5. Issues with changing business strategies to offer alternative product and services

Source: Asia–Pacific MSME Trade Coalition. COVID-19 SME Impact Survey. https://mailchi.mp/amtctrade/survey-results-covid-19-sme-impact-survey.

The massive defaults and escalating job losses of the pandemic call for well-targeted public support to provide essential financial relief to MSMEs, as noted earlier. Initially, relief aimed to ensure business continuity, preserve employment, and provide sufficient liquidity for doing business during the pandemic and ease recovery afterward (Table 19). Ongoing financial support measures must strive to be timely, timebound, and accessible for MSMEs as the pandemic enters a new phase as vaccines begin to circulate (although slowly in many developing countries). Eligibility criteria of MSMEs for various facilities should be carefully reviewed and monitored as the pandemic and the emerging vaccines to end it evolve. In the long term, governments may need to consider worst-case scenarios of defaults and debt forgiveness. The extent and gravity of losses incurred due to business closures may call for measures such as creation of funds/mechanisms for business and debt restructuring for MSMEs in financial distress. During this time, central banks need to maintain accommodative monetary policy while monitoring the effects on inflation and other variables of these policies; monetary and macrofinancial policies can support MSME access to banks and nonbank financial institutions (ADB 2020h).[19]

Table 19: Financial Assistance to Micro, Small, and Medium-Sized Enterprises during COVID-19 in ASEAN+3 Countries

Country	Capital Buffer Safeguards	Deferral of Debt Repayments	Relaxation of Lending Conditions	New Lending	Credit Guarantees	Regulatory Forbearance
Brunei Darussalam		Deferred principal payments				
Cambodia	Capital injection Base rate reduced	Debt restructuring for priority sectors		A new public bank for MSMEs		Banking sector stimulus
Indonesia	Capital buffer on banks required	Debt restructuring	Interest rate reduced by 25 bps	Max Rp10 billion loans for MSMEs		Banking sector stimulus
Lao PDR		Debt restructuring				Loan classification
Malaysia	RM3 billion for MSME loans with 3.5% interest rate cap	6-month moratorium on repayments Debt restructuring	Interest rate reduced by 50bps	COVID-19 Special Relief Facility (working capital loans for MSMEs)	RM50 billion guarantee scheme (80%)	Waiver of listing fees on capital markets for SMEs
Philippines	Base rate reduced Capital relaxed	0-day grace period for debt repayments	Interest rate reduced by 25 bps			

continued on next page

---

[19] Monetary and macrofinancial policies such as injecting liquidity into commercial banks, cutting the reserve requirement ratio to help banks to expand credit to MSMEs (e.g., the People's Republic of China), and granting regulatory forbearance, including reclassification of nonperforming loans.

Table 19 *continued*

Country	Capital Buffer Safeguards	Deferral of Debt Repayments	Relaxation of Lending Conditions	New Lending	Credit Guarantees	Regulatory Forbearance
Singapore		● Deferred principal payments		● Enterprise financing scheme expanded		
Thailand	● B0.9 trillion liquidity support measures	● Deferred principal payments ● Debt restructuring	● Interest rate reduced by 25 bps	● Soft loans/ credit lines for MSMEs		● Banking sector stimulus
Viet Nam	● Base rate reduced ● Transaction fees scrapped	● Deferred principal payments ● Debt restructuring	● Interest rate and transactions fees reduced/ waived	● Soft loan packages ● Zero interest loans for wage payments		
China, People's Republic of	● Liquidity support ● CNY800 billion extra funding by FIs for MSME loans	● Deferred principal and interest payments for MSMEs	● Interest rate reduced by 10 bps	● Refinancing facility for MSMEs with 2.5% interest rate ● Special credit quota for MSMEs		● NPL definitions
Japan				● Emergency loans for MSMEs with low/zero interest rate	● 100% guarantee scheme for firms decreasing sales	
Korea, Republic of	● Base rate reduced	● Deferred loan repayments	● Interest payments for MSME loans suspended (6-month)	● Emergency funding for business with low interest rate ● W29 trillion MSME loans	● W5.5 trillion guarantee scheme for MSMEs ● 100% guarantee scheme for small merchants	

bps = basis points, B = baht, CNY = yuan, COVID-19 = coronavirus disease, FI = financial institution, Lao PDR = Lao People's Democratic Republic, MSMEs = micro, small, and medium-sized enterprises, NPL = nonperforming loan, RM = ringgit, Rp = rupiah, W = won.

Source: ADB. 2020. *Navigating COVID-19 in Asia and the Pacific*. Manila: ADB. https://www.adb.org/sites/default/files/publication/633861/navigating-covid-19-asia-pacific.pdf.

As noted, addressing short-term liquidity was the initial immediate focus of policies. Some of the most common policy instruments included (i) tax deferment of payments remitted by businesses to the government are deferred to ease SMEs' liquidity constraints; (ii) credit availability to SMEs increased by the government through direct borrowing from state-owned banks, reduction of interest rates on loan programs, expanding credit guarantee scheme use, or extending grace periods of current loans; (iii) wage and income support for temporarily laid off workers are subsidized by the government; and (iv) encouraging a shift to other business models, services, or products. The government could also advise SMEs on how to manage their cash flows and workforces as well as guide them on their way to recovery (Vandenberg 2020). Government interventions such as public lending and credit guarantee schemes have been evidenced as the most agile countercyclical tools to deploy and facilitate the required flow of funds crucial for SMEs to reestablish and continue business operations.

Examples of rate reduction, soft loans, refinancing, and credit guarantees to improve MSME liquidity during the pandemic, that developing economies could find helpful, include tax incentives to agriculture and hard-hit sectors and credit support to SMEs and manufacturing enterprises in Kazakhstan; direct subsidies to SMEs and businesses to help maintain their employees in Armenia; the introduction of low-interest loans for SMEs with 100% government guarantee in Hong Kong, China; and deferred income tax payments in the tourism sector in Georgia;[20] rate cuts, refinancing facilities, and reductions of reserve thresholds for bank lending to SMEs in the PRC; and allocation of over ¥1.6 trillion to provide credit guarantees to MSMEs, low- and even zero-interest loans, and subsidies on "sustainabilization" investments to help sustain businesses through the crisis in Japan (Karr, Loh, and Wirjo 2020).

Historically, credit guarantee schemes have played a significant role in countercyclical relief during multiple crises.[21] As such, economies across Asia and the Pacific have swiftly rolled out credit guarantee schemes to support SMEs. The following are examples of credit guarantee schemes implemented across Asia:

- Cambodia's Ministry of Economy and Finance established a credit guarantee fund of $200 million to guarantee loans through banks and financial institutions.
- In Malaysia, the government pledged to support the private sector's growth and boost the country's economy through the introduction of a RM50 million financial guarantee scheme through the Danajamin PRIHATIN Guarantee Scheme.[22]
- The Philippine government announced a ₱120 billion credit guarantee program for affected small businesses.[23]
- In Thailand, the Small Industry Credit Guarantee Corporation signed the Soft Loan Plus Loan Guarantee Program with 18 partner banks that will provide SMEs with soft loans payable after 3 years.
- Timor-Leste extended access to the Credit Guarantee System to microenterprises, increasing the type of economic activities eligible for the program.
- The Mongolian government approved guarantees to support vulnerable businesses amounting to $39 million.
- To ease liquidity problems, authorities in Hong Kong, China provided low-interest loans for SMEs, with 100%, 90% and 80% guarantees.

---

[20] International Monetary Fund (IMF). Policy Responses to COVID-19. Policy tracker. https://www.imf.org/en/Topics/imf-and-covid19/Policy-Responses-to-COVID-19 (accessed 10 March 2020).

[21] Kim, S., H. Lee, T. Kessler, & M. Khan. 2021. Policies to Optimize the Performance of Credit Guarantee Schemes During Financial Crises. ADB Briefs, No. 167. https://www.adb.org/sites/default/files/publication/680196/adb-brief-167-credit-guarantee-schemes-financial-crises.pdf.

[22] Danajamin Nasional Berhad is Malaysia's first and only financial guarantee insurer. It provides financial guarantee insurance for bonds and *sukuk* issuances to viable Malaysian companies to enable access to the corporate bond *sukuk* market.

[23] Credit Mediation and Restructuring Guarantee Fund, an expanded loan program that will cover all "critically-impacted businesses" nationwide. Philippine Board of Investments. Financial Assistance. https://boi.gov.ph/financial-assistance/.

- The Government of Bangladesh provided a Tk20 billion credit guarantee scheme for cottage, micro, and small industries.
- In Indonesia, Rp3 trillion worth of loan guarantees for SMEs was approved.
- The Sri Lankan government provided credit guarantee to banks—ranging from 80% for smaller loans to 50% for relatively large loans—to provide loans at an interest rate of 4% using the banks' own funds.

Banks should stand ready, including to rapidly deploy business continuity plans, boost cash in hand, and avoid the debt trap of borrowing short to lend long. Shareholders must maintain their presence to boost confidence and capital for the banks to serve micro and small businesses while withstanding the impacts of the pandemic. Again, social distancing means MSMEs cannot engage in face-to-face assessments of bank loan applications. Thus, credit officers become essential workers on the front lines to perform business health checks and unlock prudent lending decisions. In addition, banks are moving toward digitization of financial services, which may require these MSMEs to embrace mobile transactions. Digitization may bring lower costs, better access, and minimal operation risk to clients when banks properly secure digitization processes. In addition to mobile payments, banks may consider using mobile wallets, web services, and other alternative channels to better serve low-income customers who have the least accessibility to digitization. Furthermore, banks can help MSMEs by innovating and expanding services to rebuild businesses that have been interrupted by COVID-19 (ADB 2020h).

Looking ahead, ADB can help its DMCs after COVID-19 has passed by promoting and developing best practices in SME lending and credit guarantee schemes. Its $6.5 billion initial package, discussed earlier, included $3.6 billion in sovereign operations for a range of policy responses and $1.6 billion budget in nonsovereign operations for MSMEs, domestic and regional trade, and firms directly impacted (WE-Fi 2020).

ADB and its DMCs also need to promote SME credit insurance solutions. Credit insurance schemes are efficient mechanisms to facilitate production and trade and add substantial liquidity in various forms into the SME market and its value chain. Credit risk insurers use sophisticated and innovative information technology-based credit risk management tools developed by the private sector. Solutions include (i) loan insurance schemes such as in Singapore, where specialized private sector insurers manage and back government SME lending and guarantee schemes; (ii) factoring insurance where the account receivables of the factors, that are purchased against a discount from SMEs, are covered; and (iii) trade credit insurance where the private insurance industry and export credit agencies protect suppliers against the insolvency and bankruptcy of their buyers as well as against political risks.

In Europe and Asia, these solutions are promoted by extending the inclusion of the types of SMEs and firms to which these schemes are open, raising the ceiling up to which the guarantee and coverage percentage applies, accelerating lending and loan guarantee and insurance procedures, and enlarging public funding available to support guarantees and subsidies insurance premium (OECD 2020b).

Fostering Digital Transformation in the Finance Sector

The pandemic has challenged financial institutions to provide more effective and convenient digital solutions for payments and financial services amid the lockdown measures and physical distancing, spurring a dramatic increase in the rate of digital adoption in financial services, as noted.

Four fundamental shifts created ripple effects in financial services: (i) it forced adoption of online, mobile, and call center channels; (ii) it accelerated the use of digital and contactless payment; (iii) virtualized workforces; and (iv) developed underlying market structure and economics. Limited mobility and work-from-home arrangements have forced rapid adoption of digital channels in financial services, massively stressing technology systems and condensing years' worth of changes into months if not weeks. Call center interactions also spiked as branches and insurance storefronts closed. Contactless transactions have increased significantly as consumers have shifted purchases online, while businesses have set up their e-commerce presence to capture sales during containment measures. Governments and firms, meanwhile, instructed workers to stay at home and work remotely. Employees and employers adjusted to meeting and working virtually using digital platforms.

As such, years of relative stability in the industry has been put to a test as the pandemic has ignited a fundamental shift in the size and structure of financial services (Deloitte 2020).

At this time, digitization continues to develop rapidly, but its success is not preordained. Policies and regulations must respond to new challenges brought by the risks in scaling up digitization while leveraging the potential of these platforms and services to accelerate economic growth and ease recovery after COVID-19.

Many digitization measures have been launched. In the PRC, MyBank, in partnership with 100 banks, has launched "contactless loans" to support 15 million MSMEs using their "310" lending model. Artificial intelligence tools help reduce risks for the lender as loan applications can be completed in 3 minutes and approved in 1 second with 0 human intervention. MiBank—a microfinance bank in Papua New Guinea focusing on women and low-income microentrepreneurs utilizing mobile services to reach remote areas with new banking services—is helping rural microentrepreneurs, the unbanked, and communities with limited access to financial services, especially in places with no physical bank branches. In Viet Nam, the Vietnam Bank of Social Policies, MasterCard, and The Asia Foundation have partnered to deploy mobile banking services to 5.1 million low-income rural clients, 51% of whom are women. In addition, financial assistance from MSME support programs sponsored by the government could be channeled through mobile money and fintech platforms (Karr, Loh, and Wirjo 2020).

ADB supported national and regional projects on harnessing new technologies to expand financial inclusion through fintech innovations and knowledge products to enable policymakers to address emerging fintech-related issues. In the PRC, ADB assisted People's Bank of China in the Expanding Access to Finance for Small and Medium-Sized Enterprises through Financial Technology Innovations project. In Kazakhstan, ADB provided knowledge and technical assistance in the project Promoting Digital Technologies for Sustainable Development. Strengthening Regional Cooperation and Knowledge Sharing on the Application of Technology in Financial Services and Promoting Financial Inclusion through Financial Technology are some of ADB's regional projects.

ADB has also implemented several digitization initiatives with its DMCs which has enabled its partners to cope with the pandemic. One such case is Cantilan Bank Inc.'s (CBI) core migration to the cloud which has paved the way for 40 other banks to receive approval from the Bangko Sentral ng Pilipinas to do the same. Due to this migration in 2019, CBI was able to easily adapt to performing remote work when the pandemic restrictions were announced in March 2020. This has also permitted them to continue their work in building their technical capacity all throughout 2020 due to the flexibility enabled by cloud technology. Today, CBI has an application programming interface layer and a mobile banking channel which allows them to respectively partner with third-party fintech players for new innovative services and expand their customer channels, allowing them to achieve scale and provide remote and convenient services for their new and existing customers.

As part of its COVID-19 response, the Southeast Asia Department of ADB, with the support of the Finance Sector Group piloted a supply chain digitization initiative in Bandung, Indonesia to enable inventory visibility for consumer-packaged goods, distributors, and wholesalers within the *warung* (tiny shops or stalls) community who supply goods and grocery to their communities. This is particularly helpful when travel restrictions are in place and supply of essentials needs to be maintained. As this ongoing pilot builds more data through digitization, *warungs*, particularly women-owned ones, will be able to utilize their data for gaining access to finance.

Among policy makers, six areas must be examined to determine country readiness to maximize innovation benefits (ADB 2020h):

(i)   Are robust identity and information and communication technology infrastructure and services available?
(ii) Are efficient trade and logistics networks in place?
(iii) Is there an efficient payment system?
(iv) Is an efficient and internationally compatible legal and regulatory framework in place?
(v)   Is there a conducive business environment for start-ups?
(vi) Does the country's stakeholders (workers, businesses, governments, etc.) have sufficient digital skills and literacy?

Thus, the finance sector must keep these policy areas in mind as digital solutions gain momentum because of the pandemic. Data connectivity, mobile technology, digital banking, and fintech can help contain the virus while promoting financial inclusion as digitization makes financial services more accessible to unserved and underserved communities.

The finance sector evolves as technology eases access to financial services such as payments, remittances, and credit. Mobile devices enable digital financial services. Fintech includes digital technologies that transform the provision of financial services to the development of new business models, applications, processes, and products (IMF 2020c).

The finance sector has been changing alongside technological advancements for decades. Emerging from this, digital financial services are providing lower costs, faster speed, better security, more transparency, and importantly, greater financial inclusion. This is especially so for the underbanked and unbanked.

The pandemic has heightened these trends, as noted. It is worth reiterating the advantages. Digital financial services allow contactless transactions; help governments disburse financial assistance quickly and effectively; and enable firms and households to rapidly access online payments and financing. Mobile money allows everyone to do remote transactions such as fund transfers, bill payments, and paying for goods and services from home (IMF 2020c).

However, as digital financial services boom during the pandemic and are quickly scaled up without the appropriate regulations and safeguards in place, risks to financial stability and integrity rise. Policy makers therefore need to hasten supervision and regulation policies to ensure a safe fintech environment for consumers and investors.

Anecdotal evidence also suggests that the pandemic can speed progress to digital financial inclusion across the globe in the long term. In 2003, for example, the SARS epidemic augmented the PRC's digital payments and e-commerce transactions (Xiao and Chorzempa 2020). In this, smooth transition to digital financial services requires sufficient digital infrastructure for access to the internet and mobile connectivity.

In the short term, however, the digital divide could widen across and within countries, as building digital infrastructure takes resources and time. Countries lagging behind on digital financial inclusion will struggle to scale up quickly, particularly with spending priorities on public health and economic support. Countries more advanced in this area, however, will enhance adoption amid high demand and government support (IMF 2020d).

Pre-COVID-19, several governments were already utilizing digital financial services to make digital payments and transfers to households and firms. Post outbreak, this trend increased as people shunned cash payments to reduce the spread of the virus. Digital payments enable payment transactions and financial support to continue without having to worry about breaching social distancing and quarantine measures. Payment of public wages and public transfers (government-to-public and government-to-business) digitally is also proven more cost-effective.

In addition, fintech improves financial inclusion of the underserved, unbanked, women, and people in the informal sector. This is especially vital in large informal sectors. Some country-specific examples include the PRC's consumption coupons, which are disbursed via WeChat pay and Alipay; as well as India's fund transfers using Aadhaar-linked accounts. Doing digital government-to-business payments, such as grants to cover wages for staff, employee retention funds for small businesses, and lending programs for businesses, also improve the speed of cash assistance. During this time, the swift transfer of funds is critical in helping developing countries respond to the health crisis (IMF 2020c).

Among country-specific examples, are wage payment digitization by Bangladesh and the Philippines (Better Than Cash Alliance 2017, 2019; Pillai 2016). In Georgia, ADB's technical assistance projects include SME lending development, deployment of tablet devices to loan officers, and simplifying credit scoring to enhance SME's access to finance (Ravelo 2017). Bypassing intermediaries and allowing direct business-to-business transactions are encouraged through distributed computing as business operations are limited due to precautionary and health measures (IMF 2020c).

Households globally are increasingly using noncash payments for peer-to-peer (P2P) transfers and in-store purchases to maintain social distancing. Moreover, governments are giving incentives to users of mobile money or e-wallets to encourage cashless transactions and contain COVID-19. In Bangladesh and India, for example, authorities are cutting mobile transfer fees and increasing transaction-size limits. Remittances are being facilitated by mobile money and digital currencies to eliminate queuing. In addition, digitization of person-to-government transactions, such as paying taxes, can raise tax collection and reduce tax evasion and corruption (IMF 2020c).

Fintech solutions also include machine algorithms that can help nonbank lending platforms and digital banks that provide lending to SMEs assess the creditworthiness of firms remotely and offer lending rapidly by automating due diligence (Bazarbash 2019). And big data analytics could help automate credit approvals, facilitating regulatory compliance, and detecting fraud. For example, fintech-based credit provision improved SME shock resilience both before and during the COVID pandemic in the PRC (IMF 2020c).

In crisis, P2P lending platforms can provide cheaper services than traditional banks. Lending software providers offer a way to quickly process loans and tap into new markets and demographics. An example is the introduction of a new P2P scheme for first-time home buyers in Malaysia. Through alternative lending platforms, households and firms can find a new source of credit, especially when a firm is small and lacks proper documentation. Contactless processing of loan applications avoids physical interaction in banks, mitigating the potential spread of the virus (IMF 2020c).

However, risks cannot be fully avoided and mitigated. Inequalities and divides may worsen as access to digital financial services continues to challenge the poor, women, residents of rural areas, and the elderly. Vulnerabilities to cyberattacks, digital fraud, and even bank runs become more pronounced as rapidly scaling up digital payments leads to system capacity constraints, unavailability of critical staff due to operating with skeletal workforces, and panics when digital financial services are linked with a social media application. Maintaining adequate know-your-customer procedures and compliance with anti-money laundering and combating the financing of terrorism measures have been a challenge as demand for digital financial services has increased. Additionally, concerns about data privacy could also arise if checks and balances provided by democratic oversight and business regulations are not properly executed (IMF 2020e).

These risks and challenges to digital financial services adoption may be eliminated if efforts to enhance the progress on digital financial inclusion are made. Measures could include the following:

- Promote and design digitization programs in businesses.
- Ensure universal access (both for consumers and merchants) to internet and mobile connectivity.
- Encourage having omnichannel payments.
- Foster an interoperable environment
- Endorse contactless transactions.
- Educate consumers about fraud and cybercrime.
- Provide financial and digital literacy to help consumers use digital financial services wisely, safely, and securely.
- Where relevant, amend regulatory and supervisory policies regarding digital financial services to safeguard financial stability, consumer protection, and competition.

Digital financial services not only contain the spread of the virus but also ease payments, remittances, and credit. Nonetheless, it should be kept in mind that risks to fraud and cybercrime are enhanced by the rapid scaling up of digital transactions. Policy makers should seize all digital opportunities that the outbreak has created while ensuring that risks to digital financial service adoption are mitigated.

Conclusion

Efforts to control the spread of COVID-19 pandemic have severely disrupted the global economy, hurting both the finance and real sectors. Initially, COVID-19 uncertainties sparked severe but short-lived financial turmoil characterized by volatile capital markets and large capital outflows from emerging markets. In the real sector, however, containment policies including restrictions on movement and social distancing have caused prolonged interruption in business activities, especially among micro, small and medium-sized enterprises (MSMEs). It also set off a massive labor shock that threatens the long-term credit quality of the banking industry.

In response to the crisis, governments have implemented an array of measures (e.g., fiscal support, policy rate cuts, liquidity support, and credit provisions) that have mitigated concerns in targeted sectors and facilitated growth in financial markets. However, emergency policies implemented to rescue the global economy have enabled the buildup of unsustainable debt and reduced credit quality, threatening long-term financial stability once government support inevitably ends.

Amid these concerns, policy makers need to promote a post-pandemic *New Normal* that is focused on balancing financial stability and economic growth with resiliency. The authorities need to strengthen supervisory and regulatory frameworks to enhance risk-management strategies during the post-pandemic growth period. Additionally, the impacts of the pandemic highlighted weaknesses and thus priority areas for reforms needed to strengthen economic resiliency to future crises. First, a disaster risk financing framework could establish domestic and regional health infrastructures to better manage crises. Second, massive capital outflows at the height of the current pandemic underscored the need for further capital market development to help with crisis fallout and exchange rate volatility. Third, the severe impact of the pandemic on the MSME sector highlights the importance of establishing wide access to MSME financing. Finally, the dramatic increase in the use of digital solutions and the benefits of digitization during the pandemic calls for development of an enabling supervisory and regulatory environment.

Appendix

Summary of Financial Market Policies in Select Asia and Pacific Developing Economies

Economy	Policies
Central and West Asia	
Armenia	• Allocated a total of dram (AMD) 25 billion (over $50 million) to cofinance loans for companies that borrow money from Armenian banks in the national currency to pay salaries, taxes, bills, and purchase raw materials. This amount includes subsidy for the interests of these of loans. • The Central Bank of Armenia reduced the policy rate three times, in May, June, and September 2020. As of 9 March 2021, the policy rate stood at 4.25%. • Provided a loan support package to small and medium-sized enterprises (SMEs) in its most-affected sectors (manufacturing, transportation and storage economy, tourism, other services sectors, and health care). The loan will be provided through the Investment Support Center of the Ministry of Economy with credit institutions acting as servicing agents for the loans. The maximum loan amount is AMD50 million, with 0% interest for the first 2 years and 12% for the third year.
Kazakhstan	• Provided tenge (T) 1 trillion ($2.3 billion) in subsidized lending under the Economy of Simple Things program. • Interest rate cut from 13%–15% to 6% for subsidized credit under the Economy of Simple Things program. • Expanded the list of eligible collaterals. • Reduced the liquidity coverage ratio requirement from 80% to 60%. • National Bank of Kazakhstan has intervened to mitigate excessive foreign exchange volatility. The central bank has been operating under an objective to stabilize exchange rates since July 2020. • The central bank cut its policy rate to 9% and widened the interest rate corridor +/- 200 basis points. • The central bank lowered the capital conservation buffer by 1%. • The central bank lowered risk weights for SME exposure in tenge (from 75% to 50%) and for foreign exchange loans (from 200% to 100%) until October 2020. • The central bank and financial institutions have agreed to allow borrowers to defer debt repayments (until mid-June 2020 the latest) as well as refrain from charging penalties for borrowers affected by the emergency.
East Asia	
China, People's Republic of	• In March 2020, the People's Bank of China announced a reduction in the banks' mandatory reserve ratio, which freed up yuan (CNY) 550 billion to support the economy. • CNY1.8 trillion was allocated for the expansion of re-lending and re-discounting facilities supporting manufacturers of medical supplies and daily necessities, micro, small, and medium-sized enterprises (MSMEs), and the agriculture sector at low interest rates. • Liquidity injection into the banking system via medium-term lending facility amounting to CNY1 trillion. • In June 2020, the central bank started to buy CNY400 billion ($56.1 billion) of loans that local lenders have provided to small businesses, which gave local banks the ability to increase small business lending up to CNY1 trillion. • The State Council encouraged financial institutions to cut the interest rates of firms. • Higher tolerance for nonperforming loans (NPL) and reduced NPL provision coverage requirements. • CNY350 billion for policy banks' credit extension to private and micro- and small enterprises. • Local governments have been allowed to replenish the capital of certain small and midsize banks as much as CNY200 billion.

continued on next page

Table *continued*

Economy	Policies
Hong Kong, China	• The Hong Kong Monetary Authority introduced measures to increase the banking sector's liquidity, encouraging banks to deploy their liquidity buffers more flexibly, and easing interbank funding conditions by reducing the issuance size of Exchange Fund Bills. • Reduced regulatory reserves to release a total of Hong Kong dollar (HK$) 1 trillion ($128.8 billion) in lending capacity. • The monetary authority engaged in repo transactions and launched a US Dollar Liquidity Facility ($10 billion) to increase banking system liquidity. • Decreased the base rate to 0.86% as of 16 March 2020. • Introduced low-interest loans for SMEs with 100%–80% from authorities. Repayment of these loans is adjusted up to 5 years (from 3 years) with an increased total guarantee commitment of HK$70 billion (from HK$20 billion). • Announced multiple payment holidays and repayment deferment of trade facilities for corporations and small businesses.
Korea, Republic of	• Bank of Korea increased the ceiling of the Bank Intermediated Lending Support Facility to a total of won (W) 10 trillion ($8.8 billion) to augment available funding for SMEs. • The central bank launched the Corporate Bond-Backed Lending Facility as a lending scheme providing W10 trillion in loans to businesses, banks, and nonbank financial institutions for up to 6 months. • Facilitated W1.65 trillion ($1.4 billion) in loans from policy banks to the auto industry as a financial aid package. • The central bank applied accommodative monetary policy including expanding the eligible list of open market operation participants to select nonbank financial institutions, expand eligible open market operation collateral list, and temporarily reducing the minimum foreign exchange liquidity coverage ratio for banks to 70% (from 80%). • The central bank lowered the interest rate on the Bank Intermediated Lending Support Facility to 0.25% and the base rate to 0.5%. • Korea Financial Services Commission recommended banks to temporarily limit dividends within 20% of their net profits until June 2021 to maintain banks' loss absorbing capacity in response to the pandemic. • The Government of the Republic of Korea announced announced a W135 trillion financial support package. Provisions of the package include: (i) expansion of financial loans and guarantees for SMEs and affected households and businesses, and (ii) creation of a bond market stabilization fund to purchase corporate bonds and commercial paper. • The Government of the Republic of Korea announced announced a W10.7 trillion stock market stabilization fund.
Mongolia	• Bank of Mongolia reduced the Mongolian togrog reserve requirement of banks to 6%. • The central bank reduced policy rates five times from March to November. Current policy rate stands at 6% (from 11%) as of 23 November 2020. • The central bank and the Financial Regulatory Commission implemented temporary financial forbearance measures on prudential requirements, loan classifications, and restructuring standards. • Announced guarantees amounting to $39 million to support vulnerable businesses. • The central bank allowed deferment of principal and interest payments for consumer, business, and mortgage loans.
South Asia	
Bangladesh	• Bangladesh Bank has allowed banks and financial institutions to borrow 360 days against additional treasury bills and bonds of statutory deposit rate with Bangladesh Bank. • The central bank reduced cash reserve ratio requirements from 5% (daily basis) and 5.5% (bi-weekly basis) to 3.5% and 4%, respectively. • The Ministry of Finance subsidized interest payments on up to taka (Tk) 500 billion in working capital loans by scheduled banks to businesses. Half of this amount (Tk250 billion) will be refinanced by Bangladesh Bank. • The central bank reduced the following: repo rate from 5.25% to 4.75%; reverse repo rate from 4.75% to 4.00%; bank rate from 5.00% to 4.00%. • Announced a Tk20 billion credit guarantee scheme for cottage, micro, and small industries. • The central bank took measures to waive credit card fees and interests, and suspend loan interest payments.

continued on next page

Table *continued*

Economy	Policies
India	◉ Reserve Bank of India has introduced (i) open market operations (over 0.1% of gross domestic product [GDP]); (ii) variable term repos (0.5% of GDP) to ease any domestic liquidity pressures; (iii) special refinance facilities for rural banks, housing finance companies, small enterprises (0.2% of GDP); (iv) a special liquidity facility for mutual funds (Indian rupee [₹] 500 billion).
	◉ Cash reserve ratio maintenance for all additional retail loans has been exempted.
	◉ The central bank temporarily reduced the liquidity coverage ratio from 100% to 80%.
	◉ The central bank introduced long-term repo operations (0.4% of GDP for the first tranche and 0.2% of GDP for the second tranche; 1–3 years).
	◉ The central bank established special refinance facilities for a total amount of ₹650 million for all India financial institutions).
	◉ The central bank extended ₹250 million to the National Bank for Agriculture and Rural Development to back agricultural operations in the wake of challenges posed by COVID-19.
	◉ The central bank reduced the following: repo rate to 4.0%, reverse repo rate to 3.35%, marginal standing facility rate to 4.65%, and bank rate to 4.25%.
	◉ It provided regulatory forbearance on asset classification of loans to MSMEs and real estate developers and introduced regulatory measures to promote credit flows to the retail sector and MSMEs.
	◉ Allotted ₹3 trillion worth of loan guarantees for small and medium-sized companies.
	◉ It provided relief to both borrowers and lenders, allowing companies a 3-month moratorium on loan repayments.
Sri Lanka	◉ Enable licensed banks to avail of liquidity through the Sri Lanka Deposit Insurance and Liquidity Support Scheme or as loans and advances in rupees under the Framework of Emergency Loans and Advances to Licensed Banks, based on acceptable collateral and liquidity forecasts.
	◉ Central Bank of Sri Lanka reduced the statutory reserve ratio from 4% to 2%, where it has since remained unchanged.
	◉ It lowered the minimum daily liquidity requirements for licensed finance companies on holdings of time deposits (from 10% to 6%), savings deposits (from 15% to 10%), borrowings (retained at 5%), and government securities (from 7.5% to 5%) up to 31 March 2021.
	◉ The Samurdhi program allowed 2.4 million beneficiaries to avail interest-free loans of up to Sri Lanka rupee (SLRe) 10,000 with a 6-month grace period and 18-month repayment period through all Samurdhi banks.
	◉ 4% working capital loan for 2 years (with 6-month debt moratorium) under the scheme "Saubagya COVID-19 Renaissance facility" for MSMEs in all the sectors, and large enterprises in the affected sectors (such as tourism) was introduced through a SLRe50 billion refinancing facility by the central bank—under this scheme, the central bank provides 100% refinancing to participating licensed banks at an interest rate of 1%.
	◉ The central bank has reduced the monetary policy rate to 4.5% (from 6.5%) for the standing deposit facility rate, 5.5% (from 7.5%) for the standing lending facility rate, and the bank rate to 8.5% (from 10%).
	◉ Permitted banks, finance and leasing companies, if required, to reclassify NPLs under the debt moratorium scheme as NPLs.
	◉ Launched a credit guarantee scheme which runs through the central bank. Under the scheme, the central bank will provide a credit guarantee to banks, ranging from 80% for smaller loans to 50% for relatively large loans to provide loans at an interest rate of 4% using the banks, own funds.
	◉ It introduced a directive for wide-ranging debt moratoriums to licensed banks, finance, and leasing companies.
Pacific	
Fiji	◉ Reserve Bank of Fiji reduced the overnight policy rate to 0.25% from 0.5% on 18 March 2020 to counter the economic impact of COVID-19.
	◉ The central bank expanded the SME Credit Guarantee Scheme to assist small entities.
	◉ It expanded credit to exporters, commercial farmers, public transportation, and renewable energy businesses.
	◉ It extended credit to commercial banks for on-lending to businesses affected by COVID-19.
	◉ It supported fiscal measures through purchase of government bonds to finance budget deficit.

continued on next page

Table *continued*

Economy	Policies
Vanuatu	<ul><li>Reserve Bank of Vanuatu reactivated the Imports Substitution and Export Finance Facility which aims to assist in improving Vanuatu's balance of payment. Under the facilities, domestic lending institutions/commercial banks can obtain low-cost, back-to-back loan/credit from the central bank for the purpose of on-lending to eligible exporters and businesses catering for import substitution.</li><li>Reserve Bank of Vanuatu reduced its policy rates from 2.9% to 2.25%.</li><li>The central bank reduced commercial banks' capital adequacy ratio from 12.0% to 10.0%.</li></ul>
Southeast Asia	
Indonesia	<ul><li>Reduced policy rates to by 100 basis points in total to 4.00%. Injected rupiah (Rp) 56 trillion to, banking industry through a term-repo mechanism with underlying government securities transactions held by banks.</li><li>Increased maximum duration for repo and reverse repo operations for up to 12 months.</li><li>Increased the size of the main weekly refinancing operations as needed.</li><li>Expanded monetary operations by providing banks and corporates a term-repo mechanism.</li><li>Reduced the reserve requirement ratio (RRR) from 8% to 4%, generating Rp22 trillion additional liquidity.</li><li>Reduced the foreign currency RRR by 4%, generating liquidity by $3.2 billion.</li><li>Relaxed additional demand deposit obligations that were intended for macroprudential intermediation ratio requirements of banks.</li><li>Raised the liquidity buffer ratio by 200 basis points (bps) for conventional banks and 50 bps for Islamic banks to be fulfilled via government bond purchases from the primary market.</li><li>Increased frequency of foreign exchange swap auctions from thrice a week to daily auctions.</li><li>Intervened in spot and domestic nondeliverable foreign exchange markets and domestic government bond markets.</li><li>Relaxed loan classification and loan restructuring procedures.</li><li>Bank Indonesia purchased Rp26.1 trillion sharia bonds in the primary market.</li><li>It purchased Rp397.1 trillion worth of government bonds at 0% interest and committed as a standby buyer for Rp177 trillion in auctions at 1 percentage point below benchmark rate. As of 18 August 2020, the central bank had made Rp82.1 trillion in primary market purchases through this scheme.</li><li>Established repurchased agreement line facilities with several institutions.</li></ul>
Malaysia	<ul><li>Provided liquidity to domestic financial markets through outright purchase of government securities, reverse repos, and reduction of RRR by 100 basis points to 2.0%.</li><li>Lowered the overnight policy floor and corridor rate to 2.0% and 1.5%, respectively.</li><li>Eased requirements for regulatory and supervisory compliance.</li><li>Reduced interest rate for the special relief facility from 3.75% to 3.5%.</li><li>Announced regulatory relief measures for publicly listed companies.</li><li>Established a ringgit (RM) 1.2 billion investment fund under the National Economic Recovery Plan (PENJANA), which will match institutional private capital investment with selected venture capital and early stage tech fund managers.</li><li>Suspended short-selling from 23 March to 30 June 2020.</li></ul>

continued on next page

Table *continued*

Economy	Policies
Philippines	<ul><li>Reduced policy rates by a cumulative 175 basis points to 2.0%.</li><li>Reduced RRR by 200 basis points.</li><li>Eased access to Bangko Sentral ng Pilipinas' rediscounting facility.</li><li>Reduced minimum liquidity ratio from 20% to 16% for stand-alone thrift banks, rural banks, and cooperative banks.</li><li>Announced a 100-basis-points cut in reserve requirements of thrift banks and rural and cooperative banks to 3% and 2%, respectively.</li><li>Relaxed documentary and reporting rules for foreign exchange operations.</li><li>Eased asset cover requirement of banks with expanded/foreign currency deposit units.</li><li>Temporary relaxation of requirements on compliance reporting, provisioning requirements, and marking-to-market of debt securities.</li><li>Deferred implementation of Basel III revised risk-based capital framework for stand-alone thrift banks, rural banks, and cooperative banks.</li><li>Allowed the use of capital buffers to absorb losses and let liquidity coverage ratio below 100%.</li><li>The central bank purchased peso (₱) 300 billion government securities under a repurchase agreement with a maximum repayment of 6 months.</li><li>It purchased ₱62 billion government securities under the expanded government security purchases.</li></ul>
Thailand	<ul><li>Reduced policy rate by a cumulative 75 basis points to a record low 0.5%.</li><li>Decreased contribution of financial institutions to Financial Institutions Development Fund from 0.46% to 0.23% of the deposit base.</li><li>Reduced interest for credit cards from 18% to 16%, and personal loans from 28% to 24%–25%.</li><li>Established the Corporate Bond Stabilization Fund to provide bridge financing of up to baht (B) 400 billion to high quality firms with bonds maturing during 2020–2021.</li><li>Purchased B100 billion government bonds to ensure normalcy in government bond market.</li><li>Signed currency swap with the Bank of Japan.</li></ul>

Sources: Reproduced, Asian Development Bank. ADB COVID-19 Policy Database. https://covid19policy.adb.org/policy-measures (accessed 8 September 2020); IMF. Policy Responses to COVID-19. https://www.imf.org/en/Topics/imf-and-covid19/Policy-Responses-to-COVID-19 (accessed 9 March 2021).

References

Adrian, T., and F. Natalucci. 2020. *COVID-19 Crisis Poses Threat to Financial Stability.* https://blogs.imf.org/2020/04/14/covid-19-crisis-poses-threat-to-financial-stability/.

Agenda.Ge. 2020. Government Announced 3.5 Bln GEL Anti-Crisis Plan. 24 April. https://agenda.ge/en/news/2020/1273.

Aggarwal, R., A. Demirgüç-Kunt, and M. S. Martínez-Pería. 2011. Do Remittances Promote Financial Development? *Journal of Development Economics.* 96 (2): pp. 255–264.

AON. 2020. The Impact of COVID-19 on the M&A Insurance Market. https://www.aon.com/apac/transaction-liability/impact-of-covid-19-on-the-mna-insurance-market.jsp .

Asian Development Bank (ADB). n.d. ADB'S Rapid COVID-19 Response in Southeast Asia. https://www.adb.org/sites/default/files/publication/631981/adb-covid-19-response-southeast-asia.pdf.

———. Calculations using data from the World Bank Migration and Remittances Data. https://www.worldbank.org/en/topic/migrationremittancesdiasporaissues/brief/migration-remittances-data (accessed December 2021).

———. 2015. *Asia SME Finance Monitor 2014.* Manila.

———. 2018. Toward Optimal Provision of Regional Public Goods in Asia and the Pacific. In ADB, *Asian Economic Integration Report 2018* pp. 121–178. Manila.

———. 2020a. *Asian Development Outlook* Supplement. June 2020. Manila: ADB.

———. 2020b. *Asia Small and Medium-Sized Enterprise Monitor 2020: Volume I–Country and Regional Reviews.* Manila: ADB.

———. 2020c. *Asia Bond Monitor:* June 2020. Manila: ADB.

———. 2020d. *Asia Bond Monitor–November 2020.* Manila.

———. 2020e. ADB, KfW Partner to Boost COVID-19 Response and Financial Inclusion in Indonesia. Asian Development Bank New release. 25 September. https://www.adb.org/news/adb-kfw-partner-boost-covid-19-response-and-financial-inclusion-indonesia.

———. 2020f. *ADB's Comprehensive Response to the COVID-19 Pandemic.* Manila.

———. 2020g. *COVID-19 Active Response and Expenditure Support Program: Report and Recommendation of the President.* Manila.

———. 2020h. *Navigating COVID-19 in Asia and the Pacific.* Manila: ADB. https://www.adb.org/sites/default/files/publication/633861/navigating-covid-19-asia-pacific.pdf.

———. 2021. *Asian Development Outlook 2021 Update: Transforming Agriculture in Asia.* September 2021. Manila: ADB.

———. 2021. *Annual Portfolio Performance Report 2020.* https://www.adb.org/sites/default/files/institutional-document/697726/appr-2020.pdf.

———. n.d. *Asian Development Bank Epidemic Risk Financing Framework for Asian Developing Countries.* Manila.

ASEAN Briefing. 2020a. Thailand Issues Third COVID-19 Stimulus Package. 2020. Dezan Shira & Associates. https://www.aseanbriefing.com/news/thailand-issues-third-covid-19-stimulus-package/.

———. 2020b. Singapore Issues Third COVID-19 Stimulus Package. Dezan Shira & Associates. 24 April. https://www.aseanbriefing.com/.

———. 2020c. Singapore Announces Second COVID-19 Stimulus Package: Salient Features. Dezan Shira & Associates. 1 April. https://www.aseanbriefing.com/news/singapore-announces-second-covid-19-stimulus-package-salient-features/.

———. 2020d. Malaysia Issues Second COVID-19 Stimulus Package: Salient Features. 7 April. https://www.aseanbriefing.com/news/malaysia-issues-second-stimulus-package-combat-covid-19-salient-features.

———. 2020e. Indonesia Launches National Economic Recovery Program. 20 May. https://www.aseanbriefing.com/news/indonesia-launches-national-economic-recovery-program/.

Avalos, F., and D. Xia. 2020. The Short and Long End of Equity Prices during the Pandemic. *BIS Quarterly Review September 2020*. https://www.bis.org/publ/qtrpdf/r_qt2009v.htm.

Awad, R., C. Ferreira, E. Gaston, and L. Riedweg. 2020. Banking Sector Regulatory and Supervisory Response to Deal with Coronavirus Impact (with Q and A). *IMF Special Series on COVID-19*. International Monetary Fund. https://www.imf.org/~/media/Files/Publications/covid19-special-notes/enspecial-series-oncovid19banking-sector-regulatory-and-supervisory-response-to-deal-withcoronavir.ashx?la=en.

Bank for International Settlements. 2018. Structural Changes in Banking after the Crisis. Basel. https://www.bis.org/publ/cgfs60.pdf.

———. 2020. International Banking and Financial Market Developments. *BIS Quarterly Review* September 2020. https://www.bis.org/publ/qtrpdf/r_qt2009.pdf.

Barajas, A., R. Chami, C. Ebeke, and A. Oeking. 2018. What's Different About Monetary Policy Transmission in Remittance-Dependent Countries? *Journal of Development Economics*. 134: pp. 272–288.

Basel Committee on Banking Supervision (BCBS). 2018. *Towards a Sectoral Application of the Countercyclical Capital Buffer: A Literature Review*. BCBS.

Bazarbash, M. 2019. FinTech in Financial Inclusion: Machine Learning Applications in Assessing Credit Risk. *IMF Working Paper 19/109*. Washington, DC. https://www.imf.org/en/Publications/WP/Issues/2019/05/17/FinTech-in-Financial-Inclusion-Machine-Learning-Applications-in-Assessing-Credit-Risk-46883.

Berger, A., and G. Udell. 2005. A More Complete Conceptual Framework for Financing of Small and Medium Enterprises. *Policy Research Working Paper Series 3795*. World Bank, Washington, DC.

Better Than Cash Alliance. 2017. Digitizing Wage Payments in Bangladesh's Garment Production Sector. https://www.betterthancash.org/tools-research/case-studies/digitizing-wage-payments-inbangladeshs-garment-production-sector.

———. 2019. The State of Digital Payments in the Philippines. https://www.betterthancash.org/alliance-reports/country-diagnostic-the-philippines-2019-edition

Biospectrum. 2020. ADB Provides $1.5B to Support Thailand's COVID-19 Response. BioSpectrum. https://www.biospectrumasia.com/news/56/16449/adb-provides-1-5b-to-support-thailands-covid-19-response.html.

Carletti, E., S. Claessens, A. Fatas, and X. Vives. 2020. Banking in a Post-Covid World. In *The Bank Business Model in the Post-COVID-19 World* pp. 16–21. London: Center for Economic Policy Research.

CGAP. 2020. *Microfinance and COVID-19: A Framework for Regulatory Response*. Consultative Group to Assist the Poor.

Chakar, M. 2020. Top Risks for the Global Insurance Industry. S&P Global. https://www.spglobal.com/_assets/documents/ratings/research/100047463.pdf.

Chatterjee, A. 2020. *How Businesses Can Stay Alive When Struck by Disaster*. https://blogs.adb.org/how-businesses-can-stay-alive-when-struck-by-disaster.

Cheema, M., and K. Szulczyk. 2020. *The 2008 Global Financial Crisis and COVID-19 Pandemic: An Examination of Safe Haven Assets*. Asia Pacific Research Exchange.

China Briefing. 2021. China's Tax and Fee Cuts Extended or Released After 2021 Two Sessions. 13 April. https://www.china-briefing.com/news/china-tax-and-fee-cuts-2021-extended-or-released-after-2021-two-sessions/.

CNBC News. 2021. Federal Reserve Leaves Interest Rates And Asset Purchases Unchanged, Sees Growth Slowing. 27 January. https://www.cnbc.com/2021/01/27/fed-decision-january-2021-rates-unchanged.html.

Congressional Research Service. 2020. Global Economic Effects of COVID-19. Washington, DC.

Deloitte. 2020. Realizing the Digital Promise COVID-19 Catalyzes and Accelerates Transformation In Financial Services. https://www.iif.com/Portals/0/Files/content/Innovation/Realizing%20the%20digital%20promise_COVID-19%20catalyzes%20and%20accelerates%20transformation%20FINAL.pdf.

de Vera, Ben O. 2020. ADB Grant Sought to Secure Learning Kits for Poor Students In Remote Areas. *Philippine Daily Inquirer*. 8 September. https://business.inquirer.net/306841/adb-grant-sought-to-secure-learning-kits-for-poor-students-in-remote-areas.

Donkin, Chris. 2020. UK, Switzerland Call for Global Remittance Action. *Mobile World Live*. 22 May.

Dryer, M., and K. Nygaard. 2020. Governments Encourage SMEs to Adopt New Technology. Systemic Risk Blog, Yale School of Management. https://som.yale.edu/blog/governments-encourage-smes-to-adopt-new-technology.

Economic Research Institute for ASEAN and East Asia (ERIA). 2020a. ASEAN MSMEs in a COVID-19 World: Lessons from ERIA MSMEs Talks 1–5.

———. 2020b. ASEAN MSMEs in a COVID-19 World: Lessons from ERIA MSMEs Talks 6–10.

El-Erian, M. 2009. A New Normal. *PIMCO Secular Outlook*.

———. 2020. The New Normal 2.0. *The Journal of Portfolio Management*.

Feher, C., and I. de Bidegain. 2020. Pension Schemes in the COVID-19 Crisis: Impacts and Policy Considerations. IMF.

Fiji National Provident Fund (FNPF). 2020. FNPF COVID-19 Withdrawal Scheme. https://myfnpf.com.fj/index.php/covid-19-updates/fnpf-relief-assistance.

Financial Stability Board. 2020. COVID-19 Pandemic: Financial Stability Implications and Policy Measures Taken.

Fitch Ratings. 2020a, August 26. Asian Reinsurers Repositioning amid Catastrophe Losses and Pandemic. https://www.Fitchratings.Com/Research/Insurance/Asian-Reinsurers-Repositioning-Amid-Catastrophe-Losses-Pandemic-26–08–2020.

———. 2020b. ASEAN Bank Exposures to Become Clearer as Relief is Tapered. *Fitch Wire*. 8 October. https://www.fitchratings.com/research/banks/asean-bank-exposures-to-become-clearer-as-relief-is-tapered-08–10–2020.

Fund-Europe. 2020. *Asian infrastructure: Adding Infrastructure to Insurers' Bow*. https://www.funds-europe.com/global-industry-2020/asian-infrastructure-adding-infrastructure-to-insurers-bow.

Furceri, D., P. Loungani, J. Ostry, and, P. Pizzuto. 2020. COVID-19 Will Raise Inequality If Past Pandemics Are a Guide. VOXEU-CEPR. https://voxeu.org/article/covid-19-will-raise-inequality-if-past-pandemics-are-guide.

FWD Insurance. 2020. FWD COVID-19 Ready. FWD Insurance Company Blog. https://www.fwd.com.ph/en/news-press/news/2020/fwd-covid-19-ready/.

Government of the Republic of Armenia, The. 2020. Action 3 in Programs to Address the Economic Impact of COVID-19. https://www.gov.am/en/covid19./.

Hayes, D. 2021. Financing The Next Generation Of Sustainable Infrastructure. *Forbes*. https://www.forbes.com/sites/forbesrealestatecouncil/2021/01/21/financing-the-next-generation-of-sustainable-infrastructure/?sh=295da7e460a7.

International Air Transport Association (IATA). 2020. Vaccines and Air Travel Position Paper. https://www.iata.org/contentassets/5c8786230ff34e2da406c72a52030e95/vaccines-and-air-travel-position-paper.pdf.

International Association of Insurance Supervisors. 2020. 2020 Global Insurance Market Report (GIMAR).

International Finance Corporation. 2020. COVID-19 and the Insurance Industry: Why a Gender-Sensitive Response Matters.

International Labour Organization (ILO). 2020a. *ILO Monitor: COVID-19 and the World of Work. Fifth edition*. International Labour Organization.

———. 2020b. *COVID-19 and the World of Work: Third edition*. International Labour Organization.

———. 2020c. *COVID-19 Crisis and the Informal Economy: Immediate Responses and Policy Challenges*.

———. 2020d. *Youth and COVID-19: Impacts on Jobs, Education, Rights and Mental Well-Being*.

International Monetary Fund (IMF). 2010. *Exiting from Crisis Intervention Policies*. https://www.imf.org/external/np/pp/eng/2010/020410.pdf.

———. 2014. *IMF Staff Guidance Note on Macroprudential Policy*. International Monetary Fund, Washington, DC. Retrieved July 27, 2020 from https://www.imf.org/en/Publications/Policy-Papers/Issues/2016/12/31/StaffGuidance-Note-on-Macroprudential-Policy-PP4925.

————. 2017. *Increasing the Resilience to Large and Volatile Capital Flows: The Role of Macroprudential Policies*. IMF Policy Paper, International Monetary Fund, Washington, DC. https://www.imf.org/en/Publications/Policy-Papers/Issues/2017/07/05/pp060217-increasing-resilience-to-largeand-volatile-capital-flows.

————. 2020a. Banking Sector: Low Rates, Low Profits? In IMF, *Global Financial Stability Report: Markets in the Time of COVID-19* (pp. 67–83).

————. 2020b. Special Notes Series on COVID-19, 26 August 2020.

————. 2020c. *Monetary and Financial Policy Responses for Emerging Market and Developing Economies*. Special Series on COVID-19. IMF Monetary and Capital markets Department.

————. 2020d. *Fiscal Monitor: Policies for the Recovery October 2020*. Washington: IMF.

————. 2020e. Digital Financial Services and the Pandemic: Opportunities and Risks for Emerging and Developing Economies Special Series on COVID-19.

————. 2020f. The Promise of Fintech Financial Inclusion in the Post COVID-19 Era. IMF Monetary and Capital markets Department.

————. 2021. Global Financial Stability Report: Preempting a Legacy of Vulnerabilities April 2021. Washington, DC.

IMF and World Bank. 2020. *COVID-19: The Regulatory and Supervisory Implications for the Banking Sector A Joint IMF-World Bank Staff Position Note.*

Isaacs, L. 2021. Remittances in Asia—The Impact of COVID-19: Harnessing Digitization to Aid Recovery in Asia. Presentation for ADB's Finance Sector Group Webinar. Manila. https://events.development.asia/system/files/materials/2021/03/202103-remittances-asia-impact-covid-19-harnessing-digitization-aid-recovery-asia.pdf.

Juergens, F., and F. Galvani. 2020. Social Protection for Older People during COVID-19 and Beyond. https://socialprotection.org/discover/publications/social-protection-approaches-covid-19-expert-advice-helpline.

Kang, J., and S. Tian. 2020. Asia's Regional Financing Woes Are Exposed during COVID-19. East Asia Forum. https://www.eastasiaforum.org/2020/12/17/asias-regional-financing-woes-are-exposed-during-covid-19/.

Karr, J., K. Loh, and A. Wirjo. 2020. Supporting MSMEs' Digitalization Amid COVID-19. APEC.

Kidd, S., D. Athias, and A. Tran. 2020. Addressing the COVID-19 Economic Crisis in Asia through Social Protection. United Nations Development Programme.

Kirti, D. and M.Y. Shin. 2020. Impact of COVID-19 on Insurers. IMF.

Knomad. n.d. Remittances in Crisis: How to Keep them Flowing. https://www.knomad.org/covid-19-remittances-call-to-action/.

Korea Joong Ang Daily. 2020. More Wages Are Covered by the Government Now. 25 March. https://koreajoongangdaily.joins.com/.

KPMG. 2020a. China Government and Institution Measures in Response to COVID-19. KPMG. https://home.kpmg/xx/en/home/insights/2020/04/china-government-and-institution-measures-in-response-to-covid.html.

————. 2020b. India: Tax Developments in Response to COVID-19. https://home.kpmg/xx/en/home/insights/2020/04/india-tax-developments-in-response-to-covid-19.html.

————. 2020c. Bangladesh: Government and Institution Measures in Response to COVID-19. https://home.kpmg/xx/en/home/insights/2020/04/bangladesh-government-and-institution-measures-in-response-to-covid.html.

Lee, J., and A. Chatterjee. 2020. The Informal Sector Needs Financial Support. Development Asia. https://development.asia/insight/informal-sector-needs-financial-support.

Lee, J., T. Kessler, and A. Chatterjee. 2020. Note on the Asian Development Bank Epidemic Risk Financing Framework for Asian Developing Countries.

Leng, C., and B. Goh. 2020. China to Inject $174 Billion of Liquidity on Monday as markets Reopen. *Reuters*. https://www.reuters.com/article/us-china-health-cenbank/china-to-inject-174-billion-of-liquidity-on-monday-as-markets-reopen-idUSKBN1ZW074.

Leng, S. 2020. Coronavirus: Nearly Half a Million Chinese Companies Close in First Quarter as Pandemic Batters Economy. https://www.scmp.com/.

Mangowal, C., E. Shukmadewi, and T. Santoso. 2020. Impact of COVID-19 to MFIs in Indonesia: A Rapid Assessment. Rise Research and Training. https://www.findevgateway.org/sites/default/files/users/user331/200518%20COVID-19%20Indonesia%20MFI%20Rapid%20Assessment_RISE.pdf.

Mayeda, Andrew. 2020. How to Rebuild from the Shock of COVID-19. IFC Insights. Interview with Mohamed El-Erian.

Medina, A. 2020. Malaysia Issues Stimulus Package to Combat COVID-19 Impact. ASEAN Briefing. https://www.aseanbriefing.com/news/malaysia-issues-stimulus-package-combat-covid-19-impact/.

Oliver Wyman. 2020. COVID-19 Consideration for Insurers in Asia. https://www.oliverwyman.com/our-expertise/insights/2020/apr/covid-19-considerations-for-insurers-in-asia.html.

Organisation for Economic Co-operation and Development (OECD). 2020a. *Coronavirus: The World Economy at Risk.* OECD.

———. 2020b. *COVID-19: SME Policy Responses.*

———. 2020c. *OECD Policy Responses to Coronavirus (COVID-19): Responding to the COVID-19 and Pandemic Protection Gap in Insurance.* http://www.oecd.org/coronavirus/policy-responses/responding-to-the-covid-19-and-pandemic-protection-gap-in-insurance-35e74736/#section-d1e322.

———. 2020d. *OECD Policy Responses to Coronavirus (COVID-19): The Impact of the Coronavirus (COVID-19) Crisis on Development Finance.* http://www.oecd.org/coronavirus/policy-responses/the-impact-of-the-coronavirus-covid-19-crisis-on-development-finance-9de00b3b/#section-d1e320.

———. 2020e. Evaluating the Initial Impact of COVID Containment Measures on Activity. OECD.

———. 2020f. March 24. Flattening the COVID-19 Peak: Containment and Mitigation Policies.

———. 2020g. March. Global Financial Markets Policy Responses to COVID-19. OECD.

OECD and ASEAN. 2020. Enterprise Policy Responses to COVID-19 in ASEAN: Measures to Boost MSME Resilience.

Oxford Business Group. 2020. Will COVID-19 Boost Private Insurance in the Philippines? https://oxfordbusinessgroup.com/news/will-covid-19-boost-private-insurance-philippines.

Pacific Financial Technical Assistance Centre (PFTAC). 2020. Annual Report 2020. https://www.pftac.org/content/dam/PFTAC/Documents/Reports/Annual%20Reports/FY2020-PFTAC-Annual%20Report.pdf.

Pacific Sector Development Initiative. 2020. Pacific Retirement Funds: Anchoring Social Protection in Good Finance. *PSDI Finance Sector Policy Paper,* Vol 2. https://www.pacificpsdi.org/publications/read/pacific-retirement-funds-anchoring-social-protection-in-good-finance.

Park, C.-Y., P. Rosenkranz, and M. C. Tayag. 2020. *COVID-19 Exposes Asian Banks' Vulnerability to US Dollar Funding.* ADB.

Parrocha, A. 2020. Palace Seeks to Send Home Repatriated OFWs within 72 hours. *Philippines News Agency.* https://www.pna.gov.ph/.

Philippine Board of Investments. Financial Assistance. https://boi.gov.ph/financial-assistance/.

Pillai, R. 2016. *Person-to-Government Payments: Lessons from Tanzania's Digitization Efforts.* https://btcaprod.s3.amazonaws.com/documents/237/english_attachments/Tanzania-CaseStudy.pdf?1515010379.

Pratt, N. 2020. Asia Institutional Investors Increase Real Asset Exposure. *Funds-Europe.* https://www.funds-europe.com/news/asia-institutional-investors-increase-real-asset-exposure.

PwC. 2020. Beyond COVID-19: Action Plan for Singapore Insurance Industry. https://www.pwc.com/sg/en/publications/assets/page/beyond-covid-19-action-plan-for-singapore-insurance-industry.pdf.

Ravelo, J. L. 2017. Adopting new technology? Here's some advice from two ADB fintech pilots. https://www.devex.com/news/adopting-new-technology-here-s-some-advice-from-two-adb-fintech-pilots-91700.

Reuters. 2020. China Will Raise Tolerance for Banks' Non-Performing Loans Amid Coronavirus Outbreak. 24 February. https://www.reuters.com/article/us-china-health-finance-idUSKCN20I0R1.

Silva, J. 2020. Crisis Is Accelerating Digital Transformation in Banking, Again. IDC. https://inthecloud. withgoogle.com/idc-financial-services-digital-transformation-20/dl-cd.html?utm_source=google&utm_ medium=blog&utm_campaign=FY20-Q3-global-jointpartner-website-wd-idc_fs_digi_ transformation_wp_q3_2020.

Sinha, S. 2020a. Has the Pandemic Spared Cambodia? Liquidity Considerations of Cambodia's Large MFIs. M-CRIL Advisory Note. http://www.m-cril.com/pdfs/20-09-17%20Cambodia%20MFI-MFbanks%20liquidity%20 analysis.pdf.

———. 2020b. A Covid Perspective on Nepal Microfinance. M-CIL Advisory Note. https://www.findevgateway.org/ paper/2020/08/covid-perspective-nepal-microfinance.

Solt, E. 2018. Managing International Financial Crises: Responses, Lessons and Prevention.

Sta. Maria, B. 2020, October 26. Four Insurance Markets Scenarios Accelerated by COVID-19. Ernst and Young. https://www.ey.com/en_gl/financial-services-asia-pacific/four-insurance-market-scenarios- accelerated-by-covid-19.

Sugimoto, N., and P. Windsor. 2020. Regulatory and Supervisory Response to Deal with Coronavirus Impact— the Insurance Sector. IMF.

Takenaka, A., J. Villafuerte, R. Gaspar, and B. Narayanan. 2020. COVID-19 Impact on International Migration, Remittances, and Recipient Households in Developing Asia. ADB Briefs, No. 148. https://www.adb.org/sites/ default/files/publication/622796/covid-19-impact-migration-remittances-asia.pdf.

Takenaka, A., K. Kim, and R. Gaspar. 2020. Despite the pandemic, remittances have kept flowing home to Asia's families. https://blogs.adb.org/blog/despite-pandemic-remittances-have-kept-flowing-home-asia-s-families.

The Hindu Business Line. 2020. Covid-19: Airtel Payments Bank Partners with Bharti AXA General Insurance. https://www.thehindubusinessline.com/info-tech/covid-19-airtel-payments-bank-partners-with-bharti-axa- general-insurance/article31268977.ece.

Tokyo Shoko Research. 2020. Impact of "New Coronavirus" on Companies Nationwide Hearing Survey. https://www.tsr-net.co.jp/news/analysis/20200309_03.html (in Japanese).

Tran, D. 2020. In Central Asia, COVID-19 Response Demands Improved Regional Cooperation. https://blogs.adb.org/ blog/central-asia-covid-19-response-demands-improved-regional-cooperation

UN Women. 2020. From Insights to Action: Gender Equality in the Wake of COVID-19.

Vandenberg, Paul. 2020. How SMEs Can Bounce Back from the COVID-19 Crisis (2020). Development Asia Policy Brief. https://development.asia/policy-brief/how-smes-can-bounce-back-covid-19-crisis?utm_ source=daily&utm_medium=email&utm_campaign=alerts.

Van der Ghote, A. 2018. Coordinating Monetary and Financial Regulatory Policies. ECB Working Paper Series. No 2155. ECB. https://www.ecb.europa.eu/pub/pdf/scpwps/ecb.wp2155.en.pdf.

———. 2019. Interactions between Monetary and Macroprudential Policies. ECB Research Bulletin. No 56. https://www.ecb.europa.eu/pub/economic-research/resbull/2019/html/ecb.rb190326~69778dd7e7.en.html.

We-Fi. n.d. COVID-19 (Coronavirus) Response Measures Supporting SMEs. 2020. Women Entrepreneurs Finance Initiative. https://we-fi.org/covid-19-response-measures-supporting-smes/.

Wei, R. 2021. Key Themes for Asian Insurance Investments in the Post-Covid World. J.P. Morgan Asset Management. https://am.jpmorgan.com/au/en/asset-management/institutional/investment-strategies/ insurance/insights/key-themes-for-asian-insurance-investments-in-the-post-covid-world/.

World Bank. n.d. SME Finance. https://www.worldbank.org/en/topic/smefinance.

———. World Development Indicators Database. https://databank.worldbank.org/source/world-development- indicators (accessed December 2021).

———. 2019. Migration and Remittances: Recent Developments and Outlook.

———. 2020a. COVID-19 Crisis through a Migration Lens: Migration and Development Brief 32.

———. 2020b. Poverty and Shared Prosperity 2020: Reversals of Fortune. Washington, DC: World Bank.

———. 2020c. Global Economic Prospects, June 2020. Washington, DC: World Bank.

———. 2020, March 29. COVID-19 Outbreak: Insurance Implications and Response. http://pubdocs.worldbank.org/en/687971586471330943/COVID-19-Outbreak-Global-Policy-Actions-on-Insurance.pdf.

———. n.d. Restructuring Paper on a Proposed Project Restructuring of Pacific Regional Connectivity Program Samoa Connectivity Project. http://documents1.worldbank.org/curated/en/904691565982098259/pdf/Disclosable-Restructuring-Paper-WS-Pacific-Regional-Connectivity-Program-Phase-3-Samoa-P128904.pdf.

Xiao, Y., and M. Chorzempa. 2020. How Digital Payments Can Help Countries Cope with COVID-19, Other Pandemics: Lessons from China. https://www.weforum.org/agenda/2020/05/digital-payments-cash-and-covid-19-pandemics/.

Yap, K., and S. Alfredo. 2020. World Bank Forecasts Philippine Remittances to Drop 13% in 2020. *Bloomberg*. https://www.bloomberg.com/asia.

Yoshino, N., and F. Taghizadeh-Hesary. 2018. The Role of SMEs in Asia and Their Difficulties in Accessing Finance. ADBI Working Paper 911. Tokyo: Asian Development Bank Institute.

Zabai, A. 2020. *How Are Household Finances Holding Up against the Covid-19*. Bank for International Settlements.

www.ingramcontent.com/pod-product-compliance
Lightning Source LLC
Chambersburg PA
CBHW050050220326
41599CB00045B/7348